Lilla S. Perry

MY FRIEND
CARL SANDBURG

The Biography
of a Friendship

LILLA S. PERRY

Edited by
E. Caswell Perry

The Scarecrow Press, Inc.
Metuchen, N.J., & London
1981

Library of Congress Cataloging in Publication Data

Perry, Lilla S
    My friend Carl Sandburg.

    Includes index.
    1. Sandburg, Carl, 1878-1967--Friends and associates.
2. Perry, Lilla S.   3. Authors, American--20th cen-
tury--Biography.   I. Perry, Edward Caswell, 1912-
II. Title.
PS3537.A618Z79   811'.52 [B]   80-21908
ISBN 0-8108-1367-X

EDITOR'S PREFACE

My mother, Lilla Perry, once said that she wished she had spent as much time on learning to write as she had devoted to studying music and learning to play the piano. She was, as she says in her preface, a "compulsive diarist." Or, more accurately, a compulsive journal keeper. When she found the time, she recorded the interesting things that came her way, but felt no need to keep a daily account, which is the hallmark of the diarist. She also wrote a lengthy account of her trip to Japan in 1936, which resulted in her obtaining many worthwhile additions to her print and other Oriental collections. I do not believe she ever attempted to have it published.

In the crunch of economic necessity following the death of my father in 1933, she found ready resource in her piano teaching, at which she was more than competent because of her ability to handle children. About 1950, she felt that she could retire, which was rather a joke, for it simply released a lot of time for her to spend on things that were more interesting to her. She could pursue her collecting interests, which lay largely in the field of Orientalia, and once again she could revert to her writing ambition.

She had at one point in her life hoped to break into the writing field, and took courses in short-story writing on several occasions. Now, fresh from her piano-teaching experience, she wrote a treatise on piano pedagogy. It was not destined to see the light of day because of the limited appeal of its subject matter, not to mention the fact that the text included innumerable plates and figures that would have been prohibitive for a publisher to reproduce.

Oriental art was quite another matter. Although there

iii

were books in fair numbers about several of her collecting specialties--Japanese prints, netsuke, inro, sword guards, and Oriental textiles--there was a conspicuous lack of material in any form about Chinese snuff bottles. At the suggestion of some of her collector friends she undertook the project of writing a book, painstakingly researching what she did not know about the subject from her collecting experience. She verified her studies on precious and semi-precious stones with the Gemological Institute, and sought the expertise of specialists on porcelain, hornbill ivory, and jade. She illustrated her text profusely with examples taken from outstanding collections as well as from her own. The manuscript was accepted by Charles Tuttle and duly published in 1960. It has been reprinted a number of times and is still in print today. To the best of my knowledge it is still the only good general account of this special area of Chinese art.

Another project Lilla Perry set for herself in the 1950s was the editing of her journals, which she converted into narrative, typescript form, embellishing the account with family letters saved over the years at appropriate points in the chronology. The final product ran to 2,169 typewritten pages of text. A little later, when the idea of writing about Carl Sandburg took shape, it was from this voluminous journal that she extracted the accounts of most of the Sandburg visits from 1918 to 1948, which formed the backbone of her manuscript. For the rest she depended on letters in her files, primarily those that Sandburg had written to her, and memory. She rewrote her manuscript several times, and in the mid-60s began sending it out to major trade publishers. In these efforts she was disappointed, and finally she turned it over to me and asked me to continue trying to secure its publication.

In this idea I was at first discouraged by the hostility of one member of the Sandburg family. But encouragement from other sources and the final acceptance of the manuscript for publication brought me to the undertaking of a fascinating editorial task. The correction of spelling, grammar, and syntax, and the verification of quotations, proper names, and literary allusions were routine, and soon I thought I was nearly finished. But the use of two untapped sources helped greatly in verifying and correcting many portions of the manuscript and filling in gaps in the chronology. The Rare Book Room at the University of Illinois provided a file of photostats of 147 of my mother's letters to Sandburg, most of which I had never seen, as she made copies of only a few. These were among the Sandburg files turned over to the University

iv

of Illinois. For acquainting me with this resource I am indebted to William Sutton and my publisher. The other resource was my mother's own extensive file of Sandburg newspaper clippings. Inspired by the harvest of data obtained from the letters, I sorted and read quantities of the newspaper clippings, thereby verifying many dates in the manuscript and correcting others. The Letters of Carl Sandburg, edited by Herbert Mitgang (Harcourt, 1968), was also helpful in identifying several people mentioned in the manuscript, and in correcting dates.

It is unfortunate that in order to protect the publisher and myself, I have had to paraphrase or omit the Sandburg letters and unpublished poems quoted in my mother's original manuscript, as thereby much of the delightful Sandburg idiom and mode of expression is lost. But I have carefully preserved all of my mother's frank comments on Sandburg and his writings as valid opinions based on an affectionate relationship of almost fifty years, and a thorough acquaintance with his literary work. The chief value of the account lies in the purely literary commentary, and here too Lilla Perry was well qualified as an intelligent, well-read individual. For the rest Sandburg's personality comes through in a series of vignettes done at various stages of his middle and later years.

I am indebted to Cole Weston for his gracious permission to use his father's 1921 portrait of Carl Sandburg. I am likewise obliged to Delmar Watson for his permission to use George Watson's photograph of Sandburg, done about 1926. The other pictures are taken from family files. I am grateful to the University of Illinois Rare Book Room for the quantities of material they reproduced for me, and for their permission to use it. I am also indebted to Kenneth Dodson for permitting me to use a portion of one of his letters to his wife, Letha, during World War II, and some quotes from a letter to my mother.

PREFACE

This story is not a biography, unless you want to call
it the biography of a friendship. If there is much in it
about myself it is because a friendship takes two people. I
have not meant this to be a biography of Carl Sandburg.
There will be many biographies of him more complete than
I could write. But my account of a friendship that spanned
almost fifty years will contain intimate glimpses, personal
reactions, carefully recorded conversations, and incidents
that few biographies may be able to provide. This should
give a vivid picture of the real man. And in my recollection
of our many encounters I am not relying on imperfect memory. My records of them were set down at the time.

I have always been a compulsive diarist. From my
earliest childhood I have been impelled to catch life in a network of words, for remembrance, or perhaps for hope of
later understanding. I have never known why I had this ob-
session to record every vital experience. I admit the obses-
sion, however, and it was always strong whenever our household had one of Carl's stimulating visits. Because of this
my book may have value for those to whom Carl Sandburg
has been a much-revered person and a symbol.

Over the years, through the public reading of his
verse, his singing of folk songs, his many television and other appearances, he became a much-loved public figure. He
was known and cherished by many who never knew a line of
his poetry beyond "The fog comes in on little cat feet, "
which they learned in school, or who never had the courage
to tackle his voluminous life of Lincoln, or his 1,067-page
novel, Remembrance Rock.

There was a time when Sandburg resented this "per-

vi

sonality cult." "Why do they want to see me? Why are they so determined to meet me, these people who never read a line that I write? Don't they know that the best of me has gone into what I have written?"

I can claim that, in spite of my fondness for him, I was no hero worshiper. I was always able to view him objectively, recognizing his faults as well as his genius. I felt, also, the need for more editing of some of his later writing. Whether he would ever have agreed to it or not is another story. Set down in a journal for my own eyes alone, this objective comment, this criticism of him or his work, seemed no disloyalty. I have wondered sometimes if my frank comments, transcribed here for the eyes of others, might not seem to his many devoted admirers like disloyalty. If that is so, I cannot help it. It was the truth as I saw it at the time. Carl himself, other than any tampering with his writing, could have taken it. I have a strong feeling that Paula, his wife, would be able to, also.

Paula Sandburg was an intellectual, with a keen, perceptive mind. Her complete devotion to Carl withheld in her any attempt to criticize or to change him. Though I believe he read her most of his writing I doubt if she ever suggested the change of a word of it. As to her influencing his actions, their daughter, Helga, expressed it well. In a magazine article about her father she described his playing with a sharp open penknife, throwing it up and catching it. It looked dangerous and she exclaimed, "Mother, can't you stop him?"

Paula's reply was the truth, I am sure, of their whole life together. "Helga, I never tell Carl what to do."

LIST OF ILLUSTRATIONS

MY FRIEND CARL SANDBURG:

THE BIOGRAPHY OF A FRIENDSHIP

Chapter I

It was in June of 1918 that Carl walked into my world.
I was attending with my husband the annual convention of the
American Library Association at Saratoga Springs, New York.
I saw him coming slowly up the steps of the enormous old
Grand Union Hotel, a relic of the fabulous horse-racing days.
I recognized him at once as the main speaker at the program
I had just heard.

Carl Sandburg was a new free-verse poet just coming
into considerable fame. He was tall, erect, athletic in build,
with a rugged face and dark hair. One long lock fell down
across his forehead. At the moment he wore the wide
visored cap by which we were to know him for years to come.

In the tremendous hall in which the recent program had
been given, few voices carried. It was before the days of
the microphone, and we had suffered through the mumblings
of the previous speakers. Then Carl Sandburg's rich, reso-
nant, effortless voice rolled out in the reading of his poetry.
No one I had ever heard, except William Jennings Bryan, had
such a carrying voice, and his was comparable in strength,
but not in quality. Carl Sandburg delighted the listening librarians.

I have no remembrance as to how I introduced myself
as I went forward on that hotel porch to meet him. We were
soon seated there with seemingly endless things to talk about.
I had just read his second book, Cornhuskers, and had known
his Chicago Poems as well. I recalled to him with laughter
the stir in New York City his "To a Contemporary Bunk-
shooter" had made. The magazine in which it had first been
printed had had to be withdrawn from the subway book stalls--

1

fine advertisement for an unknown free-verse writer! It was a merciless tirade against Billy Sunday, a well-known evangelist of the day. In the poem came the line "What do you know about Jesus?"

"Yes, " he said with a broad grin, "and the publishers had made me tone that down a bit. As originally written I had it 'What in hell do you know about Jesus?' "

"I remember the extraordinary review Edgar Lee Masters gave to that first book of yours. " I replied. "I believe your publishers used part of it on the jacket of Chicago Poems. There are a few phrases of it that I can even now remember. "

> He puts words to the uses of bronze. His music at times is of clearest sweetness like the tinkling of blue chisels, at other times it has the appropriate harshness of resisting metal.

Mr. Sandburg's blue-grey eyes showed interest that I had remembered that review. Those were the days when I remembered everything that interested me. Lost as all such writings are lost in the world of criticism I begged to know whether Mr. Sandburg had the whole of the Masters review.

"It is possible that someone in the family may have kept that review, " he answered. "In those days favorable reviews were precious. I'll send it to you if we have it, " he added.

We gossiped about other free-verse poets I had been hearing at the Friday Morning Club in Los Angeles. At that period women's clubs throughout the country were in their heyday. Today, fifty years later, I, who no longer belong to any club, wonder what has happened to them. They no longer seem to be considered newsworthy in any way, and their influence politically is never mentioned. Fifty years ago their status was quite different.

The Friday Morning Club, the second-largest woman's club in the United States, had a membership of more than three thousand and was run by a group of the keenest, best-informed women I had ever met. I told him what a social and intellectual vacuum I had found New York City to be, when, as a stranger, I went there to live after college days at Cornell University. Los Angeles, where we went when

2

my husband became director of the Los Angeles Public Library, was a mentally stimulating place by contrast. This was largely on account of this group of exceptional women into which I had been quickly drawn. It was they who had been bringing free-verse writers and other literary people to the Coast. We had had Vachel Lindsay, Edna St. Vincent Millay, Max Eastman, Sherwood Anderson, Alfred Kreymborg, John Masefield, and William Butler Yeats. It was a long roll of illustrious names I reeled off for him. But I was seeking to impress him and to lead up to my question.

"If I were to get you three program engagements in Los Angeles, would you feel it worthwhile to come to the Coast?"

"Indeed I would," was his answer. "Amy Lowell has told me that for some unaccountable reason there seems to be much more interest in free-verse writing on the Pacific Coast than there is in the East. It is something experimental and new. The West has never been as tradition bound as the East."

"Free verse," I said, "has been a constant subject of discussion in our club groups. It's controversial. Many do not like it, and refuse to call it poetry. But it has its advocates, too. At any rate, it gets read. Many of us have been influenced by Harriet Monroe's enthusiasm for your own work. Wouldn't you say her Poetry Magazine is the best outlet for poetry in the country just now?" As he nodded agreement, I continued. "Wouldn't you say she is its most discriminating critic? Her review of your first book, Chicago Poems, in 1916, was a review which compelled even the most reluctant free-verse poetry readers to take you seriously. Surely you kept her reviews," I said. "If you find that you have, and will send them to me with the Masters review, I promise to get them back safely to you," I added.

While discussing these reviews and the group of women I had found in Los Angeles I was searching around in my purse for our last club bulletin. I had found no time as yet to read it, but a few paragraphs on the front cover had caught my eye. "Let me read you this as a sample of the kind of mind I find among these women," I said. "This was written by a recent president of the club, Josepha Tolhurst.

Is the Friday Morning Club worth while? Only as long as it remains critical and democratic. This

3

is not easy. Our very prosperity is a menace.
Things overgrown become spongy, seedy and taste-
less. To protect the democratic temper we must
be severe, independent, ironic, cool and combative.
Tolerance is an amiable virtue, but greater is
discrimination. We may find it wise to use some
discrimination in regulating our membership. As
for me, I would maintain the financial requirements
at the lowest consistent with safety, but I would
raise the literacy test. And I would fine everyone
who utters a platitude or who applauds one.

I had just finished the reading of this aloud to him when
my husband came in search of me. It was nearing dinner
time. The two men talked for a few minutes, hitting it off
well from the start. I was pleased when Everett asked Mr.
Sandburg to sit at our table. He realized that our speaker
was alone and that he probably knew very few people at that
convention. It was an era when we all "dressed" for dinner
and we agreed to meet in the lobby in half an hour.

When we did appear later arrayed in evening clothes
Mr. Sandburg, of course, was still in his blue serge suit,
but that bothered neither him nor anyone else. Come to
think of it, in all the years I knew him I never saw him in
anything but a business suit. A tuxedo would have seemed
incongruous somehow. In his later years he did appear on
television in evening clothes, but it is told of him that he
rebelled at putting on cap and gown when given his honorary
degree at Harvard.

There were only eight or ten at our table, but conversation was not general. From a distance I noted that our
new friend was rather quiet, though he held his own well in
the talk that went on. It was mostly about the war. Things
were not going well with us overseas.

After the dinner the group at our table scattered.
There was dancing in the big ballroom. Everett and I, keen
about dancing, were on the floor until they dimmed the lights
and played the "Home Sweet Home" waltz, always the final
number in those days. I can remember Sandburg standing
for a time in a doorway watching, but he did not dance. We
walked toward him once between numbers and Everett said,
"May I loan Mrs. Perry to you for a dance?" "Sorry,"
Sandburg answered, "I think I'd like it, but I never learned
to dance."

4

When Everett and I had gone to our room we talked him over. We were in agreement on the wonderful program he had given that afternoon.

"Somehow," my husband admitted, "when he read those poems they seemed extraordinary. I'd like to hear every one of them again. That one which begins 'I am an ancient reluctant conscript,'--wasn't that a gripping thing! Somehow when I brought his book of poems home I didn't think much of them. I haven't been really sold on free verse. But today, hearing them in that wonderful voice of his, there seemed plenty of rhythm and I never missed the rhyming."

Then we got to discussing his appearance. "One of the reviews says he is forty-one years old," I commented. "He is tall, isn't he?"

"No," Everett replied, "I doubt if he is more than five feet ten, two inches shorter than I am. It's his erect bearing that gives that impression. He stands tall, and he's not one pound overweight. Let's try to get him off to luncheon or dinner by ourselves tomorrow. The group tonight was too large for us to get much out of it. Did you find out whether he is staying over?"

"Yes," I answered, "He's staying over. I suspect the American Library Association is putting up for all the expenses of its main speaker, besides his fee?"

"Yes, of course," Everett answered.

There were several good talks between Sandburg and ourselves before the convention was over. I was impressed with his telling that he had made his way from Elmhurst, just out of Chicago, to Saratoga Springs, New York, a distance of about eight hundred miles, entirely on the network of trolley cars that bound the Eastern towns and cities together at that time.

"It was a wonderful way to see the country," he told us.

I had a suspicion that, with five-cent fares for long distances, it had been a very economical way as well. I should have asked him how long it had taken him, but I didn't.

If he were to remember me at all out of those convention days I have an idea it might be for a question I asked that brought forth his booming laughter, which was in later years to become so familiar to us. In the midst of a lot of my highfalutin talk about his free verse I had suddenly turned upon him with the question, "But Mr. Sandburg, how do you earn your living?"

When his roar of laughter had subsided he replied, "I'm a reporter on the Chicago Daily News."

Chapter II

On my return home to Los Angeles it would have
been easy to arrange programs for Carl Sandburg with our
three largest clubs.   But he could not come at that time.
Writing was always more important to him than speaking engagements.   He had to be caught for such things "between
books," as it were.   His answer to my first letter reveals
that.   With that letter he sent the Edgar Lee Masters and
Harriet Monroe reviews that I had requested.   Masters had
reviewed Chicago Poems as follows:

> He is an observer with sympathy but without fear,
> compassionate, but with an epic restraint, thought-
> ful without a synthetic purpose, and comprehensive
> of a vast spectacle of restlessness, aspiration and
> pain.   He puts words to the uses of bronze.   His
> music at times is of clearest sweetness, like the
> tinkling of blue chisels, at other times it has the
> appropriate harshness of resisting metal.   He de-
> rives from no one, sees with his own eyes,
> touches with his own hands, is hearty, zestful,
> in love with life, full of wonder, fundamentally
> naive.   He looks calmly on great blackness, pover-
> ty, sordidness, abject misery, hopeless agony,
> but with the self-possession of an artist.   He loves
> stormy water like a Norseman, and the blue skies
> of Olympus like a Greek.   He has Slavic gaiety
> for pastoral delights and the natural reactions of
> healthy flesh.   He is a comrade of great loneli-
> ness, has outstared Fate that thwarts, is a friend
> of Death as Nature's doorman at the house of
> Life.   His book is sound, daring, inclusive of
> many types in the city, and makes a contribution

7

to American literature of emancipating influence, and of permanent importance either in itself or its effects.

Harriet Monroe had written of Sandburg and his Chicago Poems in this vein:

> Carl Sandburg has the unassailable and immovable earthbound strength of a great granite rock, which shows a weather-worn surface above the soil. Like such a rock he has a tender and intimate love of all growing things--grasses, lichens, flowers, children, suffering human lives. His book, whether you call it poetry or not, is fundamental in the same majestic sense of the wind and the rain. It is a man speaking with his own voice, authoritatively like any other force of nature.
>
> I remember the emotion with which I first read many of these poems--typewritten sheets sent to Poetry early in 1914. That first conviction of beauty and power returns to me as I read them again. This is speech torn out of the heart because ... of the incommunicable loveliness of the earth, of life, --is too keen to be borne; or because the pain of the "poor, patient, and toiling, " of children behind mill doors, of soldiers bleeding in the trenches--all the unnecessary human anguish--is too bitter for any human being, poet or not, to endure in silence.

Elsewhere Harriet Monroe had said:

> What Sandburg does is not, as some students seem to infer, the complete sweeping away of the metrical pattern. There is an underlying three-time or four-time beat in each poem, his preference leaning, oftener than with most poets, to four-time, which admits that generous use of spondees-- sometimes four long syllables in succession--from which he gets his most telling effects. But in his underlying pattern, Sandburg permits himself more variety than the prosodic laws have allowed for, especially in the number of syllables to the bar, and in the free use of rests.... To say that there is less art in such manipulation of rhythms than in following accurately, for example, the exact metrics of a sonnet is simply to show one's own limitations as a student of poetics. It makes no dif-

ference whether the art is conscious or instinctive. With Sandburg it is probably instinctive; he may not know a spondee from a kilowatt, but he has a marvellously sensitive ear. He listens for his rhythms over and over, and beats them out with elaborate care. None of the scholarly imagists or other free versifiers of the present period has so greatly widened rhythmic range of English poetry; and the prosodists of the future will have to study him in order to make new rules to enslave poets yet to come.

Sandburg's letter accompanying the reviews was a wonderful one, written in longhand as all his first letters were. A few years later a young friend of my oldest son, Richard, appealed to me for a Sandburg autograph. I went carefully over a sheaf of Sandburg letters I had kept, and chose this first one as a gift to him because I thought it the most revealing of the man. I parted with the letter reluctantly. But the young man, Grover Jacoby, had aroused my liking and interest because he was himself writing poetry. I was sure the letter would mean much to him. The joke of it was that a number of years later when I looked over his autograph collection, I found that he had cut off that letter and kept only the signature!

Sometime late in 1920 I must have appealed to Sandburg again to come to the Coast to give us some programs. In his reply of December 13, 1920, from Chicago, he expressed his appreciation for the kind of letter I had written, and his vivid recollections of the two days at Saratoga Springs. Had I called the house in Chicago, when traveling through, I would have learned that he was off for Stockholm. He put me off as to any programs because of several big jobs he was busy on, but referred me to his agent, Mrs. M. J. Stevenson. He suggested that his old pal Rube Borough, now on the staff of the Los Angeles Record, could be helpful, and he expressed his interest in a future program. He hoped that it would go over and that he could meet me and my truly vigorous group.

Chapter III

_____

    With Mr. Sandburg's first West Coast visit now in
the offing, Everett and I discussed asking him to make his
headquarters with us. We both wanted him. "But when you
invite him," my husband suggested, "at least give him a picture of the kind of household he'll be getting into, with five
oftentimes tumultuous children all over the place. There are
people who couldn't take it, you know." There were: Richard, ten and a half; Caswell, eight and a half; Dorothy, my
adopted daughter, eight; Norman, five; Beatrice, two and a
half.

    In my invitation for him to stay with us I gave a
facetious picture of our exuberant household, ending "If
you've got the courage to try it, we want you."

    Along came his reply from the editorial rooms of
the Chicago Daily News, dated January 14, 1921. He thanked
me for my invitation, and said he expected word from Mrs.
Stevenson about dates in March. He expected to enjoy a home
with healthy, rambunctious children around, and anticipated
meeting my woman's group.

    On February 25 came a note confirming the fact
that he would have programs to give in March, and asking
that I make no dates for him except for meeting Rube Borough and Charlie Chaplin. While he would like to meet some
of the groups and people I had mentioned, he would talk
about definite dates later. He expected to arrive March 6,
and would wire a confirmation.

    On March 4 came a telegram announcing his arrival
at Williams. He planned to do the Grand Canyon on Satur-

10

day, and would arrive at Los Angeles on the Santa Fe, 2:40 Sunday afternoon, the 6th. He suggested that I make dates to meet my friends on the following Tuesday afternoon and evening.

He arrived at the old Santa Fe railway station, a small country-town station that was the best Los Angeles had to show at that time. It was almost three years since I had seen him, but I recognized him at once, from the moment he stepped off the train, by the visored cap he wore. I made no apologies when I took him home on the street car that ran from the station to within half a block of our house. Few people had automobiles in those days. I was sure he had none himself. We sat in the front open section for he wanted to smoke. That smoking was a strange procedure. It amused me, though I made no comment on it. He took out a cigar and cut it in two with his pocket knife. One half he smoked until there was nothing left to hold onto, then he lit up the other half. It was a little ritual that never varied in all the years I knew him.

He entered into our family life as if he had indeed left one just like it. Beatrice, now almost two and a half, was the same age as his third and youngest daughter, Helga. I suspect he played with her in much the same way. He would make horns over his head with his hands and come toward her while she wriggled with delight. Again and again he got Norman and Dorothy to dance for him. They had a clowning routine that tickled him. "The Christie Comedies will get you yet!" he laughed.

That first visit was unlike the others that followed over the years. On most of them he would be working at something, closing himself away from people because of the necessity to get writing done. On that first visit he was "between books." He was curious to see what these people on the West Coast were like. He was interested to find out why they seemed to be a little more receptive to new ideas than in some other parts of the country. He let me have all the parties I wanted. We used to say that, during that first visit, literary Los Angeles streamed through our doors.

One night Rupert Hughes appeared. Hughes was at the height of his writing career at this time. Occasionally he wrote music as well. He had written a musical setting to one of Sandburg's poems, and Sandburg asked him to sing it. Rupert Hughes took off his coat, took off his collar and tie--his wife laughingly said if there had been time he would have unlaced his shoes--then sat down at the piano and made the rafters ring with his musical version of "Chick Lorimer." I think Sandburg liked it, or wanted to understand it, for he asked Hughes to sing it a second time.

I recall an afternoon when only three of us were sitting before an open fire. Sandburg came down the stairs with a sheaf of manuscript in his hands. He wanted to try something out on us. The two women with me in front of the fire were Dorothea Moore and Katherine Smith. Dorothea Moore had written and published some excellent verse herself. She was the former wife of Charles F. Lummis and had later married Ernest Carroll Moore, the Provost of the University of California at Los Angeles. Lummis had been well known in the Southwest as a writer, as the former Los Angeles city librarian, and as the founder of the Southwest Museum. Katherine Smith was head of the literature department of the Friday Morning Club, and a member of Everett's library board.

Sandburg read us his first version of a poem on the Grand Canyon. We three listened appraisingly and critically. Then for some time we fought unavailingly to get Sandburg to remove one word we didn't like. He had used the word "spit," only one degree more or less poetic than the word expectorate, we told him. We couldn't move him. Just at that point in the verse he needed a gesture of some kind, he said. "Spit" did it.

A few months later came my inscribed copy of Slabs of the Sunburnt West. In my reply, which I tried to make as telegram-like as his own communications, I wrote: "Have read the book. Delighted! So glad to find you took the spit out of the Grand Canyon!"

At that same gathering of us three he had told about his visit to the Canyon. In a little alcove in the hotel there had been gathered all that had been written about the Grand Canyon. Pretty poor stuff, he thought. There was one writer, however, who really seemed to get the feel of the place. His name was Charles F. Lummis. Sandburg had never heard of him, he said. There sat Dorothea Moore, Lummis's former wife. She never looked up nor spoke.

At a larger gathering one afternoon during that first visit one daring spirit among the women spoke up and complained, "But you never write any love poems, Mr. Sandburg. I thought poets always wrote love poems."

Sandburg looked at her meditatively for a moment. "Perhaps I've written them, but maybe I've written them just for myself, without any intention of publishing them. There is one entitled ''Troths' which I put in Chicago Poems that you might call a love poem." Sandburg then recited the five lines, dealing with memories of yellow dust on a bumblebee's wing, the lights in a woman's eyes, the red in the changing sunset light, asserting that even death could not cheat him of some of these recollections.

Though the Perrys had no automobile as yet, many of our friends seemed to have one, and Sandburg was called for and driven to all his programs. He had recently been made motion-picture reviewer of the Chicago Daily News and on a number of evenings his friends in Hollywood came and got him. I had given him a key to the house, so we never knew when he got in. He kept a newspaperman's hours, I am sure, for he never appeared for breakfast the next morning until eleven or after. At that irregular hour I got his breakfast myself, not wishing to disturb the cook's routine. Mother and I joined him in the coffee, or made his breakfast our lunch time.

Since my father's death Mother divided her time between our home and my sister's place in New York City. Though my household was well staffed with help, it was wonderful to have Mother on hand to supervise everything whenever Everett and I went off on trips.

These breakfasts were to me the most interesting occasions of his visit. One morning he told us of his evening with Charlie Chaplin. Chaplin had done some takeoffs the night before that Sandburg described so well that we laughed through a great deal of the breakfast. Together with the autograph he had given Sandburg, Chaplin had drawn a caricature of himself with hat, shoes, cane, and gloves. It was so clever a thing it showed how many-sided Chaplin's genius must be.

Once when Sandburg was opening his mail he flipped a note from the Bookman across to me with a check for fifteen dollars in it. "They have just bought a poem of mine on which I have been whittling for more than a month."

13

There were a few evenings when there were no guests and we had him all to ourselves. Everett's pleasure was great at the times when Sandburg would get out his guitar and sing the many folk songs he had been collecting. There were favorites: "There's a Man Goin' Round Takin' Names"; "Look Down, Look Down Dat Lonesome Road"; "The Boll Weevil." He also sang many of the seldom-heard Negro spirituals.

Sandburg had brought no guitar with him. On one of the first mornings of his visit he had asked me to direct him to a music store. He came back with a guitar, which was returned when he left. I don't remember that he ever brought a guitar with him to use at his programs.

We didn't know, when Sandburg played and sang for us in the evenings, that, hidden round the corner of the stairs, three little figures--Richard, Caswell, and Dorothy-- were huddled close to the wall, listening. It was usually long past their bedtime hour, but this was something they could not miss.

If he felt in the mood he would let loose sometimes on some terrible jail songs, which he said he seldom sang: "God Damn Your Eyes," and others. I never heard him do them in later years.

It was good to have him with us. We were sorry to have him go. Soon there came the only note that ever followed a visit. Sandburg's thank-you letter of April 15 was a chatty one. His return to his own household reminded him of the Perrys--all the hubbub, the cries, and the music. He spoke of sending on some of his books and hoped to see some of my writing. He asked to be remembered to Everett, Dorothea Moore, Katherine Smith, and others. He enjoined me, if I ever took someone to meet Mrs. William De Mille again, to be sure to let them know that she is the daughter of Henry George. He mentioned that the Chaplin poem had been drafted, and he had found songs in Texas and Tennessee.

Chapter IV

In June of 1921, only a few months later, I went East again, leaving four of my children in Mother's care. My husband wanted me to take two-and-a-half-year-old Beatrice with me. She was a curly-headed, blue-eyed little darling, and he wanted his mother to see her. On our return trip I stopped to visit dear friends in Hinsdale, Illinois. It was but a short distance from Elmhurst, where the Sandburgs lived, and I had written Sandburg telling him when we would be there. There came a most welcoming phone call. "If your friends can't drive you over, I will bicycle over to see you. But I'd really like you to see my outfit here though, if you can."

My friends drove me over. They were people whom Sandburg might well have liked to know, having their own distinction. Their thrill at having a chance to meet Carl Sandburg, shows clearly the place and name he had made for himself even at this time.

Sandburg met us at the gate on our arrival, excused himself to my friends and took me into the house to meet Mrs. Sandburg. She was ill in bed at the time, he told us.

My friends should have recognized this as a dismissal, but perhaps they were too eager to see something more of him. They left the car and seated themselves in the garden to await our return. Margaret, Sandburg's ten-year-old daughter, played hostess to them and to Beatrice. When she came to me at her mother's bedside to tell me that my friends were still there she tactfully added that her father had some work to finish and would not be downstairs until later. I went back to the garden, repeated Margaret's explanations and saw my friends on their way.

Margaret struck us at that time as a very precocious youngster. My friends as well as I were impressed with her grown-up manners and her conversational gifts.

I find the following account of that first visit in my journal:

> Bidding goodbye to my friends, I went back to Mrs. Sandburg. She was having some sort of trouble requiring her to lie flat on her back. She told me what it was, but I have forgotten. She was no invalid, she declared, and would be glad if I would stay and talk with her. She was a slender, worn-looking little woman with most beautiful eyes, a deep blue with long lashes. To myself I called them fringed-gentian eyes. Her grey hair lay in little ringlets around her face. It was a delicate, lovely face.

We were getting on famously when in a short time Sandburg himself reappeared. He asked what I thought of the stories he had sent Margaret to give me to look over. She hadn't given them to me. When questioned she said, "But how could I, Daddy? Mrs. Perry was visiting with Mother. She couldn't look at them then!"

Margaret was forgiven and the stories produced. That was what Sandburg was working on at the time, getting ready a volume of children's stories.

"Would adults care for them?" I asked.

"If they don't I shall consider the stories a failure. They must allure but baffle children."

"Read one of them to Mrs. Perry, Carl."

While he read, Mrs. Sandburg lifted herself on her pillow and watched him with smiling eyes. He kept glancing at me for approval at the good spots. Later, however, when he talked about San Francisco and his adventures there after leaving us in Los Angeles in the spring, he looked at her as he spoke, and they seemed to be talking things over together. Again and again, as my questions set up new trains of thought, he would turn to her and say, "Oh, I forgot to tell you--"

"But San Francisco! San Francisco!" He let himself go at the name and then followed a catalogue of its charms, of its physical features, rolled out in his rich, vibrant voice, with a rhythm that made it seem like a bit of his own free verse. "About San Francisco there is the intangible, the ineffable, the something that Los Angeles will never have in a thousand years. Los Angeles is to San Francisco what Berlin is to Paris, or (he turned with a smile of some special meaning to his wife) what Moscow is to Stockholm."

I spoke of my own thwarted attempts to see San Francisco again since living on the Coast. I had seen it once on my wedding trip. "When I plan a trip there the children always come down with measles or something," I laughed. "Dorothea Moore," I told him, "has asked me to go there with her some time. She and Dr. Moore had been living there at the time of the great earthquake and lost every possession they had in the fire."

"Yes," he said slowly, "seeing San Francisco with Dorothea Moore would be really seeing San Francisco!"

We spoke of Edward Weston's pictures of him taken in Los Angeles. I don't know how great Edward Weston's fame as a photographer was at that time, but he had called me up and begged me to use my influence or my husband's with Sandburg to let him take some pictures of Sandburg.

"Why should I?" said Sandburg, "I've been mugged enough by my brother-in-law, Edward Steichen, who is the finest impressionistic photographer in America. He was head of the photographic division of the expeditionary forces sent to France in 1917."

He weakened, however, at my request and let Weston take some photographs. Weston had sent his results to us as well as to Sandburg.

Mrs. Sandburg then suggested that Sandburg show me some of the pictures her brother had made of him. As he turned on the lights in a front room, I stook before a picture which made me catch my breath, a photograph of Sandburg and his wife. I was so impressed by it that they gave me a glossy reproduction. It lacked the quality of the original, but served to help me remember it. It showed the two heads, his and hers. The clear strong lines of both sug-

17

gested a bas-relief, or a thing sculptured. It showed you
the spirit of two people: his, the spirit I had partly known;
hers, now revealed to me suddenly, completely, without the
need of further hours. There were tears in my eyes when
I went back to her where she lay.

"My brother, Edward, thinks it is the best thing he
has ever done," she said. "It does seem, somehow, to
express the very spirit of us. Life has been hard for us.
We have had to hew our way. But not everyone gets that
picture as you do. Some of our friends have objected that
Brother did not make me pretty. Life hasn't been pretty for
us. And it is astonishing, too, that people who love verse
and who know art, too, do not get that picture. It did not
impress Amy Lowell when she was here."

My response to the picture seemed to create a bond
of understanding. There were many other fine pictures of
Sandburg and herself, but none like that one. She showed
me other photographs of her brother's in Camera Work, a
magazine edited by Alfred Stieglitz. There were pictures of
Isadora Duncan, Yvette Guilbert, Grover Cleveland, Charlie
Chaplin, "the man who looked like Erasmus," and several
of Rodin.

Her brother had lived for a time with Rodin, she
told me, and was the first man who ever had an exhibition
of photographs at the Paris Salon. "He was only twenty years
old then," she added.

Sandburg then came back with some manuscripts for
me to look over. Among them was a Charlie Chaplin sketch,
which I did not like. He saw my doubt about it and said it
was only a start. There was much more to be done with it.
The others I had hardly time to glance at, for he began some
new folk songs he had gathered since I saw him last. We
did not get far, for at the sound of his singing the children
came trooping in, Beatrice and little Helga with Margaret.

While I was seeing my friends off in the garden Margaret had brought out her baby sister just awakened from her
nap. I understood at once what Sandburg had kept exclaiming
about at our house. Little Helga was just one month older
than Beatrice, but of exactly the same weight and the same
height. Add to this that they both had yellow curly hair,
combed or uncombed the same way, blue eyes, and round
baby faces, and you had an identity in appearance that revealed differences only to a discerning parent.

18

To see those two clasp fat little hands and make off for a sandpile with Margaret was a sight I would not willingly have missed. Mrs. Sandburg was now seeing them for the first time and they delighted her. We watched them as they played together near her bed.

"Point by point, features, coloring, everything, aren't they amazingly alike!" I exclaimed.

"Yes, but Helga has a slightly Scandinavian look that Beatrice has not," she replied.

"From your side or Mr. Sandburg's?"

"From Carl's."

We watched those two little backs and curly, gleaming heads bent over the sandpile in the garden again. Had I not known the yellow rompers of mine I could not have told them apart at that distance. There was plenty to amuse them. There was the sandbox with all kinds of dishes, there were wildflowers all over the garden that could be picked in bunches, there were chickens and two rabbits, and best of all, an affectionate, long-suffering dog named Prints.

"His original name was P-r-i-n-c-e," Mrs. Sandburg explained, "but we changed it to P-r-i-n-t-s, feeling we wouldn't be quite at home with royalty."

Was it any wonder that, until the guitar and folk songs temporarily lured them, the children had no thought of us, nor we of them? Janet, the second daughter, was away with friends for the day. I did not see her on this first visit.

At that moment Mrs. Sandburg's mother, a neatly dressed, quiet little woman, called us to supper. "Ah," she said quaintly when her son-in-law introduced us, "This is a friendly young face!"

"Friendly, but not young," I laughed.

As we left Mrs. Sandburg's bedside she said, "It is our maid's day out, and I am helpless, as you see, so you will understand that we are not entertaining you as we would like, Mrs. Perry."

"No fear about Mrs. Perry's understanding," Carl assured her.

We dined sumptuously on a large dish of macaroni and cheese and plenty of milk. Sandburg had declared earlier that he was going to make the coffee, but we had been too busy talking. Now he warmed up coffee in the pot, and drank three or four black cups. He invited me to have some but I preferred the milk.

It was now nine o'clock. Beatrice had gone wild about the dog and was hard to restrain. It was time to go. There was no time for me to play the piano for Mrs. Sandburg, as Carl had earlier requested that I do. He especially wanted her to hear some Cuban dances that I had played for him at my house, strongly rhythmic things that he had called for again and again.

He carried Beatrice over his shoulder to the station a few blocks distant and put us on our train. As we walked along the tree-lined streets I burst out, "Why didn't you tell me you had such a wonderful wife?"

He laughed aloud. "What do you expect a feller to do--holler about it?"

In a letter of July 18, which had not reached me in New York in time, he had suggested that I come to the office of the <u>Chicago Daily News</u> and go with him to a Poets' Luncheon given by Harriet Monroe. This day at his home had been better.

On February 28, 1922, Sandburg wrote a letter that gave evidence that he was still living in the Rootabaga world of his children's stories. It was all in the vivid imagery of those stories, the shimmering castanets, castanet clicks, blue rabbits, and the Village of Cream Puffs in a high careless wind, and was signed: Boll Weevil.

Chapter V

In 1924 there came another visit from Sandburg. I
had not known he was arriving this time until there came a
voice over the phone in the words of one of his old folk songs.
"This is the Boll Weevil a-looking fur a home." The unforgettable voice. There was always room in our big house and
my reply, I am sure, made him feel welcome. He walked
in upon my husband at the library, I remember, and they
both came out home together.

Carl's agent had a chain of engagements for him,
and wherever he could he was collecting folk songs for his
American Songbag. A Mrs. Rickerby, wife of a former professor at Pomona College, had written him saying she would
like to turn over to him her late husband's entire collection
of folk songs. The Perrys had no car at this time to take
him to Pomona, but one of our friends sent her chauffeur and
limousine to take him there. It was a full day's effort and
when he returned I remember one of his comments on the
day's adventure that brought a laugh at our dinner table.

"You know," he said, "sitting there in that luxurious
car with a chauffeur up in front I said to myself, 'How come!
A proletarian poet in a plutocratic palanquin!'"

His visit was rich in events and stimulating talk but
my account of it is lost. Hunt as I have through all my
journal pages I cannot find it. My surmise is that I had the
temerity to send it on to him after he returned home. It
went with some stories that he had asked for. He probably
never returned it. But I do recall from that visit his treatment of our mutual friend, Katherine Smith. He had accepted an invitation to lunch with her and a protégé of hers

whom she was trying to encourage in his writing. The opportunity to meet Sandburg would have meant a lot to that young man, she knew. I was aware of her invitation and that she was planning to pick Sandburg up at my house at one o'clock.

He and I were sitting over breakfast, involved in the wonderful talkfest that always came at that hour, when I realized that the clock hands were moving on toward one. Some comment he made led me to realize that he had no intention of keeping that engagement. I was sorry for Katherine. Her plans were carefully made and she had a reservation, I knew, at the best restaurant in town.

I slipped away from the table and on an extension phone upstairs asked her to call and remind him. When he was summoned to answer the phone a few minutes later I heard his reply. He could not keep the appointment, he said. "I'm working. When I am in the midst of a piece of work I have to bash my best friend in the face." Poor Katherine, I am sure, felt sufficiently bashed. Returning to the breakfast table, neither he nor I mentioned the matter, but he sat for an hour more with me and talked leisurely.

In my account of the many events of that second visit I had included this story of his treatment of Katherine. I knew it was there, but I did not care. This was the last visit when he did not seem to mind the stream of visitors who came to the house at all hours to meet him. He was still deep in the garnering of folk songs and ready at any moment to pick up his guitar and try out new ones on us, or answer our calls for the old favorites. Many an evening I was aware that three of the children were around the bend of the stairs sitting quietly in their pajamas listening. Like them, I thought it well worth their while and said nothing.

Sandburg was still motion-picture reviewer for the Chicago Daily News at this time. As on his previous visit, the movie studios sometimes sent their car for him, and he visited the studio lots. He generously included me in these expeditions. It was fun: it was still the day of the silent films, and we watched the taking of scenes.

On the day of his departure I remember we came in from a walk to find my rooms burgeoning with flowers. They had arrived in our absence, and Mother had taken them from their boxes and arranged them. I turned upon Carl with an exclamation, for I could not imagine who else had sent them. Actually they were from my friends, who wanted to express their appreciation to me for having shared him.

"Lilla Perry," Carl exclaimed, "for all your hospitality and courtesies to me, I should have sent them. But I didn't! Truly embarrassment causes more suffering than crime."

I thought that a good exit line.

Portrait of Carl Sandburg by Edward Weston and Margarethe Mather, 1921

Chapter VI

In 1926 I went on with Everett to another library convention in the East. I always lengthened my own stay by two weeks to see my friends. Mother, as always, looked after the children and the running of my household. In August, once again I visited my dear Hinsdale friends, and was driven over to see the Sandburgs in Elmhurst. This time my friends did not leave their car. They planned to return at five to pick me up.

Mrs. Sandburg met me at the gate. Again I noted her young face and lovely blue eyes. They seemed to look at you always with a smile in them. She introduced me to a woman friend whose name I have forgotten and announced that Carl was busy finishing a piece of work and would be down at four.

Meanwhile, it appeared we were to stroll in the garden. It was a stifling, hot day. I had a coat on my arm, and a very heavy portfolio of Japanese prints, which I was taking to show some artist friends with whom I was to dine that night. I wondered if I were to sense everything through the haze of an agonizing headache, which had come upon me on the drive over.

The garden was a barren-looking spot, demanding, Mrs. Sandburg said, a heavy toll of labor for small returns. I wandered toward the porch with my burdens, for I was hot and tired. If there had been any other moment for seeing the Sandburgs, I should have given up this visit at the gate. Something of my distress must have shown in my face, for after about fifteen minutes of conversation Mrs. Sandburg suggested that I take my things into the house.

At the door we met Mr. Sandburg. "Why, Carl, are you down already!" his wife exclaimed. "I explained to Mrs. Perry ..."

"Yes, but I heard her voice, and had to see her at once," he said cordially, grasping my hand and arm in a hearty way that almost cleared my head for a moment. He had grown grey, and looked older than when I last saw him.

"Can't you find something for Mrs. Perry to eat? I don't believe she has had her dinner," he said, as he drew me into a sort of porch dining room. The remains of a meal stood on the table. It was three-thirty, and I protested that I had eaten. I would, in fact, have liked to have closed my eyes while the clearing away of the crumby dishes went on before me. It was that damnable headache.

Perhaps Carl may have felt I was in the wrong mood for them, but it was like him a little to make matters worse. Sitting astride his chair with his arms on the back, he inquired, "Well, how is Los Angeles? Tell me the last news of the Iowans, and about Aimee Semple McPherson." Aimee Semple McPherson was the notorious evangelist of her day.

I am afraid my eyes flashed. "The only interest I have discovered in Aimee Semple McPherson has been since I arrived in Chicago," I lied. "And as for the 'Iowans,' why need they bother anyone?" I asked tartly. "You escape them always by as much as there is in you that is not Iowa. Why do we always dub dull people 'Iowans'? (That was true in California at that time.) Such people exist everywhere. To whom of them did I introduce you?" I asked, still belligerently.

Sandburg saw I was angry and it seemed to amuse him mightily. He gave one of his infectious laughs. "Well, that's a fact. You didn't introduce me to any, Lilla Perry. There weren't any Iowans in your bunch. How is Dorothea Moore? And Katherine Smith?" Sandburg disclaimed having received Dorothea's book of poems that I certainly had sent him.

Mrs. Sandburg had learned from me in the garden what I had in the portfolio I was carrying and asked if I would show them the Japanese prints. I was glad to. I had just had marvelous good luck in New York City and acquired some of the loveliest Utamaros that I had ever seen. It was

25

hard for an ardent collector to imagine anyone indifferent to them, but Carl certainly was. He usually expressed a reaction. This time his silence expressed one.

He brought out an armful of what he called Chinese paintings and squares of tinted paper he had found on Grant Avenue in San Francisco. We sat for twenty minutes looking them over with more serious attention than had been given my old wood block masterpieces. His were tourist stuff. The papers had tinsel designs and colors that rubbed off on your fingers. He insisted on giving me a sheet. I watched him closely for any sign of his perpetrating a joke, but no indeed, he was serious.

I was glad when he offered to sing us his new folk songs. This time, however, he took a terribly long time tuning his guitar, the dog kept rushing through the rooms, the children after him, and when we did get the new tunes they seemed to be in an experimental stage. It was almost incredible that he should try them out on me. Then he started a blasphemous one, laughing down Mrs. Sandburg's expostulations. "Oh Lilla Perry won't be shocked. She has a look as though she might be but she won't."

I called for some of the old-time favorites. Mrs. Sandburg had risen to leave us for a moment. "Just wait a minute till I get back," she asked. "I haven't heard these for a long time."

"When Carl sings, Paula can forgive him anything," remarked the family friend, who was still with us.

"I'll wager she's had plenty to forgive," I mischievously added, and drew from Carl (still strumming) a more meaningful glance than I had expected.

The strumming went on and on. I wanted him to do something well or stop. It became unbearable. There was hope my friend's car might be at the door and I rose to go. I felt as though I had been struggling in a vacuum. This time I had somehow established no real contact with them.

We had a few more words as we stood on the porch, "People keep asking me what I am working on now," Sandburg said, "as if a fellow didn't have to have a little while to catch his breath before tackling a new job. I usually say I'm writing a dissertation on Diogenes."

26

"Why didn't you try that on me a while ago when I made the same bad break?" I inquired.

"Ah, one doesn't do that to anyone who has been as nice to one as you have, whose latchkey one has possessed, and whose house one has had the run of."

"What a cruel restraint!" I laughed as we shook hands.

Mrs. Sandburg walked with me to the waiting car and we visited there for a few minutes. The eldest daughter, Margaret, the charming ten-year-old of several years ago, appeared now for the first time. I had been much taken with her on that earlier visit. She was about fifteen now.

"Whose car is that!" I exclaimed suddenly, beholding one in the yard that I had not noticed before. "Does Carl Sandburg have a Ford!"

"What else would Carl Sandburg have but a Ford?" laughed his wife.

"Does he drive it?" I questioned curiously.

"I drive it," she continued. "Once a year Carl takes a lesson on how to drive it, forgets everything for a year, and then takes another lesson!"

So ended this Sandburg visit.

Chapter VII

In early February 1929 we learned through the papers that Carl Sandburg was booked for programs in Los Angeles. We were sure to get a phone call soon that he was here. Because there was time for anticipation I learned for the first time what his visits meant to my children. No house guest ever made so much of them. He listened so respectfully to their stories and charmed them with his own. They could hardly wait until he arrived.

To Richard, my oldest son, now in college, his visit was going to mean more than to any of us. Out of his enthusiasm for Sandburg he was at the moment preparing for his manuscript club an article on him, "Sandburg, the Man and the Writer." He had reviewed Sandburg's recent book, Good Morning, America, for his college paper. He had done it so well that Dorothea Moore had said it looked as though he were bound for the doom of being a writer himself. Richard had sat on the edge of my bed and read aloud to me almost every poem in the new book, and burst out with the exclamation, "And just to think, Mother, when Sandburg was here, in this house, I let him get entirely by me!" More than once I was made aware he did not intend to let that happen this time.

Carl's phone call came from the railroad station. Was there a corner in my house he could call his? When I assured him there was he said an old newspaper friend, Dunning, had met him and they were to have dinner and do the town. Did it matter that he could not tell me just when he would arrive? I assured him it didn't.

It was ten o'clock when Sandburg, with his friend Dunning, rang the doorbell. Mother and I were sitting reading before a lively hearth fire. Everett, worn and tired as he always seemed to be those days, had gone upstairs to bed. Richard had reluctantly kept a date made days before with Pauline, his current girlfriend. It was for a sorority dance. He was hoping, he said, to get home early.

Sandburg greeted us warmly, putting his arm tenderly around Mother, of whom he always made much. "You know, Dunning, it wouldn't seem natural to camp anywhere when I'm in Los Angeles except with the Perrys. Isn't this my third visit? I feel at home around here. They know my ways. They let me come and go. They make no plans for me that I have to tie in with." Then he paused and said thoughtfully, "There are a few people I ought to see while I am here."

"Do you want me to gather them here for you?" I asked. "I could do it easily, without any trouble at all. Afternoons, perhaps. Everett isn't well, and on account of his condition, as I wrote you, I have drawn in from my own social activities. Do you remember your first visit?" I laughed, and so did he.

This time it would be different. No one would be asked to meet him. This was partly because it fitted in with my own present way of life, and mostly perhaps (since Katherine Smith's experience with him) I had realized how impossible he had become for any sort of social maneuvering. It wasn't only in literature that Carl had done for years what an old drunken playwright had said of him out on the movie lot. He had slapped Sandburg on the back, exclaiming "By Gawd, Carl, all your life you've done exactly what you wanted to do, and by Gawd, you've got away with it!"

In speaking of this later, however, Carl had said to me, "It may possibly be true, but do you know, Lilla Perry, no one has ever been as surprised that it should be so as I have myself."

My one safe course was to attempt to do nothing with him or for him, to let him alone, unless I wanted to find myself with jaw dropped and hands empty. Meanwhile, as a detached human being of whom one asked nothing, he was a rich study and source of enjoyment.

We enjoyed him now, as he sat before the fire, telling of his search for his Lincoln material for the new Lincoln book. He tried out chapters on us, humanizing and dramatizing events of those early Civil War years. One chapter was captioned with a newspaper headline: "The South has seceded." He raised the curtain on a scene in Washington the day the news came. Sometimes his deep voice sank so low Mother could hardly catch his words. Sometimes he shouted till we feared for the sleepers upstairs. The Lincoln material at the time was his chief absorption. He overflowed with it the entire visit.

He had three books for me that he had picked up in the bookstores that day: Poems of Walt Whitman, to which he had written the introduction; Literary Lights, by Gene Markey, a book of caricatures; and Orientations of Ho-Hen, by T. K. Hedrick, from which he read aloud choice bits with deep relish. While Mother and I talked with his friend Dunning, he wrote in the front of each book an inscription for the Perry clan.

Sandburg was now fifty-one. He looked much older, but was still very erect and active in his movements. His heavy thatch of hair, hanging carelessly over his forehead, was now almost white. His grey eyes, sometimes blue, never penetrating except when they contracted in laughter, seemed focused more than ever on the far horizon. Many times he stopped midway on a sentence, and you waited wonderingly until he came out of his dream. The tempo of his speech, always slow and unhurried, seemed slower than ever. I wondered how Dorothea Moore, with her leaping staccato thinking, would ever endure this. He would die someday, sitting motionless in a garden with his back against some old sun-drenched wall, his eyes fixed forever on those far distant horizons into which, for all his writing, he has never been able to take us. I thought this because I have seen him thus in my own garden, talking to me with wider and wider spaces of silence, till at length I knew he had withdrawn from me wholly.

I was impressed more than ever this first evening with the marvel of his voice. Untrained, he did with it things great actors and singers seem unable to do. Those who did not like his poetry admitted they always liked things they had once heard him read. He created rhythm entirely independent of accent. His speaking voice played with tone. I have heard him say "Chicago" on three degrees of pitch when he wished to convey a certain meaning. He dropped or raised his pitch on certain words to convey what others needed to convey with a gesture. He never used a gesture, for his voice was full of them. If voice were all, he might have been one of the greatest actors. Probably he might have been a great singer as well, for without a vocal lesson in his life he made himself acceptable to a wide public as a singer of folk songs.

That was the first evening. At about twelve-thirty, after Dunning's departure, Mother and I took him to his room. From then on his visit swung around in about the same circle it had done before. He came downstairs in the morning between eleven and twelve, and some mornings sat as long as two hours over his coffee, talking.

About one or two o'clock some of his newspaper friends would call for him and we saw no more of him till he let himself in with his own door key. It would be anywhere between twelve-thirty and two. If any of us chanced to be up he sat down and might talk for two hours more before he withdrew with his glass of milk and two graham crackers. Oftener, however, the house was dark and the only knowledge we had in the morning that he had returned was his closed door.

His time was spent going over Lincolniana collections, of which there were more than one in Los Angeles, and in second-hand bookstores hunting Lincoln material. At this time Sandburg was doing a series on the talkies for the Chicago Daily News.

Part of our morning sessions with him was a report of the doings of the day before. He missed no chance to be with Charlie Chaplin. "He's a great genius. He is funnier over a supper table with two or three friends than he ever is on the films. And to see that fellow work! To see the faculty for infinite pains he has in him! We watched him on the lot yesterday. There was a scene where a blind girl puts a flower in his buttonhole. He had it done over nine times, talking to her, directing her patiently all the time. At supper Chaplin took off the deaf-mute Mexican who works around the place. This man has his own symbolic gesture for each person he refers to, this --for Chaplin himself, --this for Sid Chaplin, Charlie's brother, --this for Sid's wife. Of course Chaplin bettered the Mexican, and for me to try to imitate for you Chaplin's imitation is--well, it's like trying to play the piano with mittens on."

31

I asked him again the first morning if I should gather in for him the friends he wanted to see. He had especially mentioned Dorothea Moore. "I tell you that book of hers, Selvage, has some of the real stuff in it. Those lines she calls 'Old Age.'" His mind had retained them with the ease with which he catches his folk-song lines:

> A little grey ape has come
> to stay with me,
> Sitting close in the shadow
> of my shadow.
>
> Shall I disguise him with a
> red coat and gold braid
> Or introduce him to everybody
> by his real name?

"I saw by the paper that Charles Lummis, her first husband, is dead. But then, I don't suppose he meant anything to her any more."

Again I reminded him of his wanting to see Dorothea. "And," I questioned, "how about Katherine Smith?"

His eyes came quickly back from their distance and an odd expression came over his face. "No, no, there is a petulance there ..." He paused for a number of seconds, then burst out, with briskness, "I have troubles enough under my own hat!"

He had not been kind to Katherine. She had made the mistake of asking something of him. I had been sorry for her. But I was not judging him. I was interestedly observing him.

Once or twice during his visit we got to this subject of the people he wanted to see, or ought to see. He ought to call up or see Mrs. Clarence Dykstra, he said.

"Wasn't she the Mrs. Rickerby who handed over to you all the folk songs which her husband had collected?" She was the wife of Clarence Dykstra now, the Provost of the University of California at Los Angeles since Dr. Moore's retirement. "I could run you around to her house in twenty minutes. And Dorothea's house is on the way." He still looked doubtful. "Or I could ask them over some afternoon."

"Oh, I don't know. I'm doing a lot of work out here this trip. I spent three hours yesterday going over books. If I get myself tied up with a lot of engagements I shall want to rush out and grab the first train."

I dropped the subject from then on.

Those breakfast hours were my time. One day when Mother came in to join us she had some photographs in her hand. They had been taken of me when I graduated from high school and when I graduated from college and a few later ones. I suspect she was rather proud of them. I had noticed it seemed to grieve her to see me looking older. Once in a while she would bring home from her shopping some miracle-working cream for the face, and once some little patches that you pasted on your forehead to smooth away character wrinkles. I doubt if I ever had time to use them.

Carl took the pictures in his hand and looked at them carefully.

"That," he said, "is a very dangerous woman!"

We laughed. How like him to get off the unexpected and surprising comment. Carl and the platitudinous were far apart.

I had explained to him that nothing but the falling in of the roof could interrupt or interfere with my daughter Dorothy's morning practice on piano and violin. Though we closed off the music room, it went on all the time he was here, and was often the softened accompaniment to breakfast. Once he knew she had finished working, he would call out requests. Manuel De Falla's "Cubana" was one. "The Tides of Maunanon," by Henry Cowell, was another. He loved to thunder forth the terrific poem that had inspired Cowell to write that.

He had always given Dorothy a great deal of attention. "You made a perfectly safe bet when you adopted that child," he said to me one morning. "You may not make a musician of her, either pianist or violinist, but she is going to burst forth in some line or other. There's a touch of genius about her. Maybe she is like Harcourt, my publisher, who had a great-grandmother who went crazy after she was fifty. She used to be found pacing up and down her garden walk, saying to herself, 'I am the most beautiful queen in the world! I am the most beautiful queen in the world!' Any of us who ever amounts to anything has had a great-grandmother or somebody with a queer twist in her brain. I think there is someone like that back of you, Lilla Perry." Somewhere in the midst of our talk about Dorothy he said, "There are bonds that are stronger than the umbilical cords."

One day we talked about interviewers and I reminded him with laughter of Alma Whitaker's interview with him the last time he was here. Alma Whitaker was a well-known writer on the Times staff. "I suppose, Mr. Sandburg," she had said sweetly, "that your most popular verse, the one by which you are best known, is that about the monkeys? 'How many monkeys are you?'" she had quoted, mentioning Alfred Kreymborg's verses. Sandburg hadn't corrected her.

"The worst interviewer I ever had," he said, "was once down in Louisiana. I had said to her, 'When a colored man gets rich he stops singing.' She quoted me as having said, 'When a colored man gets any money he's no good.' I am thankful when they pull out pad and pencil, and take down exactly what I do say."

Dr. Albert Shiels, our superintendent of schools, had been at the house the evening before. I tried to characterize him and to recall choice ironic bits that unfailingly came from him whenever one was with him. Among others I quoted the remark he had made when we were waiting for Everett in a hotel lobby one day. A throng of women going to some convention (as the cards on their lapels indicated) filed through, and he turned to me and said, "One woman may be adorable-- but aren't fifty horrible!"

Sandburg laughed heartily, "That's a mighty good line!" he agreed. "But then, I've noticed that you know a good line when you hear one."

On this slight encouragement I ventured to bring out a notebook of Grover Jacoby's verse. Grover was the seventeen-year-old friend of my son Richard, in whom I was interested.

I read him first five lines called a Cinquain, the little verse form developed by Adelaide Crapsey. It had been a problem set for a poetry class. I thought he had done well with it.

> Our souls
> Are but wild winds

34

That raise the dry grey dust
In stinging clouds that whirl and then
Subside.

Absolute silence. Embarrassing silence. I looked at him and saw he had no intent to speak.

"Perhaps that seems to you imitative and so valueless. But doesn't all work begin with imitation?" I asked.

"Yes, it's imitation. I should consider something primitive and spontaneous more promising."

I tried another, dealing with the lamentable fact that even great beauty lived with and dwelt upon loses its stirring power:

Some flashing spark has caught my eye,
Soon all is put to rout,
For with a dull and dwelling glance
I've stared its beauty out.

I read the last two lines again. "Those are good lines," I asserted.

"Yes," he agreed, "those are perfect lines, but the rest has to be worked up to them."

I made him listen to one more. I knew he would say it was artificial, but of its kind I still believe it showed promise of better things.

Thralls of the Day

From quiet thrones wrought from the
    cool and ebon night
The stars are thrust into the furnace
    of the sun,
Who welds them all into the golden
    bars of light
Which fills the sky until the burning
    day is done.

"Poetry of youth," was his comment. "Five years from now he may not be writing or even reading poetry at all. Oh, I have such quantities of verse sent to me. Unless it is outstanding, I have to send it back without comment. I

35

used to bother a good deal with young writers, advising them, trying to help them. But I find they peter out in the vast majority of cases. "

I asked him about our friend Jake Zeitlin, for whose book of verse Sandburg had written an introduction.

"Judging from his new stuff which he read me the other night, he may be going to peter out, too. I found him surrounded by Rockwell Kent's things. He's getting too 'arty.' "

"When I find nothing for me in Rockwell Kent I think there is something the matter with me, maybe," I commented.

"When I can't find anything in Rockwell Kent, I know there is nothing the matter with me, " he laughed.

More than once during his visit he talked to me about some diary pages I had sent him. "You have a gift for that kind of thing, " he said; "the real human stuff is in them. They are clean cut, trimmed down. In reading them I can't skip a word. "

One night I left on his dresser a half-dozen more "diary pages" with a little note. "This is the book open at another place. Maybe these wouldn't go over as the others did. "

The next morning he was even more expressive about them. "How much of that kind of writing have you got?" And without waiting for me to answer he went on, "I wish you would let me show them to Harcourt, my publisher. He'd see them as I do. He'd want to do something with them. "

"They couldn't be published until the people involved in my story are gone, " I answered.

"Names could be camouflaged. Otherwise they would go just as they are without retouching. Do you mind if I keep these?" he asked. "I was so sleepy last night when I came in that I wasn't intending to read a thing. But I read your pages through twice. "

To give him some idea of the amount of material he had sampled I went up into the attic to my trunk and brought down an armful of books (they were as much as I could carry) and piled them high on a couch. The earliest pages were written when I was thirteen.

"These ought to be in a safety deposit box, safe from fire," he said. "Take out your bonds," he smiled, "and put these books in. I'm serious," he reiterated, "they should be in a safe place."

One morning my son, Richard, who had slept late, had breakfast with him. "What are you intending to do with yourself after college?" Sandburg asked.

Of course Richard did not know at that time, and one of us asked what had been Sandburg's own first step after he had finished his Lombard College days.

"I went into the fire department in my own home town, Galesburg, Illinois, and drove a fire engine for two years while my family, my relatives, and friends looked on in disapproval, and asked what I was ever going to do with my education. They were considerably bothered by my failure to make use of it. I had my own idea about it, however. I had chosen the one occupation I could find, which at the same time that I earned my living, permitted me to cover a wide course of reading which I had laid out for myself, unassigned by any university. And you see, except for the two hours a day spent in exercising the horses--good healthy outdoor work--I was free, my time was my own."

"Did your mother understand? What were her feelings about you at this time?"

"I don't like to recall my relations with my mother during that period. My mother's satisfaction in me rose as the public began to approve of me more and more."

One morning we were speaking of the Dr. Dolittle books, and the fact that Hugh Lofting has never written in any other line. "That is where I've got Lofting beaten," he said smiling broadly. "When they tell me I don't know how to write poetry, I go off in a corner and write a children's story. When they tell me my children's stories are no good, I join the bearded historians. If they slam me as a historian I can walk into any newspaper office and they'll say to me 'Get busy there. Go get this interview.'"

His friend Dunning usually called for him around one.

Once as they were leaving the house Sandburg said to him, "You should see Lilla Perry in the work she does around here with her children. I've never seen anyone who came up to her as a mother except Mrs. Sandburg. They are both great environmentalists, each in her own way."

"Carl's a wonderful ego-booster," I laughed. "Sometimes I think I'm a terrible mother!"

On the last evening he came home early--early for him. It was 10:30. One of the university professors and Pauline, Richard's girlfriend, were here playing bridge with Everett and Richard. I had just served refreshments and we were talking when his key turned in the lock.

He had promised to sing folk songs to the children, and I went up and wakened them as I had done once before on a previous visit. They had been expecting the summons and came down in a moment, slipping their bathrobes over their pajamas.

There was a call for old favorites: "Three White Horses"; "Stacker Lee"; "Look Down, Look Down, Dat Lonesome Road"; "There's a Man Goin' Round Takin' Names"; "Boll Weevil." They wanted even the old Negro spirituals they have heard over and over on the victrola records. They asked for all that they knew, and he threw in a few that were new. Richard had heard from us so much about his terrible blasphemous jail songs that he asked for them after the little folks had been sent off to bed. But Sandburg shook his head. He had to work up to them. The mood and the group had to be right.

On the whole, to Everett and me, his singing of the folk songs was not equal to what he had done before. He was absorbed now by another subject. Folk songs were not his prime interest, now that his American Songbag was out. He was at times uncertain of words, and the old sureness and zest were missing.

After one of the songs his voice trailed on in comment on it, and little ten-year-old Beatrice, burst out, after she had gathered the meaning, "Why, Mr. Sandburg, I thought you were still singing! I thought that was part of the song!" There was all that tone and rhythm in his speaking voice.

After our guests left Everett went off to bed. Only

Richard and I lingered in front of the fire with Sandburg. He
was to leave the next morning, and as long as he wanted to
talk we were glad to forget time with him. It was two
o'clock when we went to bed.

It was characteristic of him that, on the search as he
was for Lincoln material, he managed for one reason and
then another to sidestep going to the Huntington Library. He
thought when he came that he wanted to go. Everett made
several engagements for him but he broke them each time.
"Anyway, the material there is unorganized and inaccessible
as yet" was his comment. Not so, as Everett knew.

When he came to leave, only Mother and I were in
the house. He put his arms around Mother and kissed her
on both cheeks. In his goodbye to me, too, there was a
warmth of feeling as if, after all these years, I had become
a real person to him. He thanked me for the comforts of
his visit. I think he meant the protection from people. He
spoke of his earliest visit. "We were having such a time
making both ends meet that the saving of hotel bills meant a
lot to me on that visit. You took me in then as the pioneer
families took in the circuit-rider--for the love of the Lord!
Next time I come I won't be working. We'll have people
again, and make it a party!"

But we never would. Nowadays people tired Everett,
and Sandburg would always be working.

In November of that same year I find this correspondence between us. Sandburg had for some time been urging
me to send my voluminous journal to his publishers. He
believed it to be a real human document and that it should be
preserved.

November 13, 1929

Dear Carl Sandburg, --
I never wrote to thank you for interesting Harcourt in my stuff. I appreciate it, though I seem
to have done nothing about it. Yesterday I received
another letter from Harcourt prompted in part, he
said, by a fine weekend visit from you. I owe you
some accounting so I send you a copy of my reply.
I wish I might take the wonderful chance you've
opened up for me.
I was in Parker's bookstore the other day.

"Sandburg's Lincoln is still selling," he commented. "A steady call for it. It's the best life of
Lincoln that's ever been written. No other can
touch it." I told him you were working on the
War Years. "Well," Mr. Parker said musingly,
"he can't ever do it again. In these first books
he dealt with a part he's strong on--folkways. He
won't be able to handle the War Years in that fash-
ion."

I tell you this because when I heard such comment once before, you said, "Why didn't you tell
me?" These things don't bother you. They get
your dander up!

A few weeks ago Richard brought me a pile of
longhand script. It was about eighty-five thousand
words, he said. He had been working all summer
on it, sometimes late at night, in the effort to
compete for a three thousand dollar prize offered
by College Humor Magazine for the best novel of
college life written by a college student. If his
father had known that he had a project of that kind
he would never have insisted that Richard take a
job in a law office for the summer. Richard had
just ten days now, he said, in which to get the
thing typed and mailed in to the Chicago office of
Doubleday Doran. The pages were too interlined
and corrected for us to turn any part of it over to
a stenographer. So I had to turn to and help him
out. He borrowed a second typewriter and we sat
side by side out in the garden and worked on the
thing eight and ten hours a day. Sometimes when
my day had been too interrupted to help him much
I worked downstairs at night until one or two in
the morning.

He got it off airmail at the last minute. Knowing the style of College Humor stories neither he
nor I think that he has much chance for the prize,
but though I never saw the whole of it, and can
judge only from the sections which I typed, I was
astonished that he had done so well. I asked why
he did not let us know what he was doing. But
there were subtle reasons no adult mind could
grasp why he "just couldn't."

I didn't mention this to Mr. Harcourt among my
other alibis for not working on the Journal. But
you know how it is for me--one thing after another.
I've no doubt Mrs. Sandburg, to some degree, has

much the same experience.   Lucky we like our
job! Remember me to her, and to yourself a host
of warm best wishes.

Yours, gratefully,
Lilla Perry

November 29, 1929

Dear Carl Sandburg, --
Since my promise to Mr. Harcourt that I would
have something to submit to him in three months I
have retreated each day for a time to my corner
of the attic.   The hardest part was the getting
started.   Now I am running along swimmingly, but
I'm not at all sure that the water's fine.   I'm having lots of fun, for I have never read over any of
this early journal stuff.   Mother and I laugh sometimes until the tears run down our faces over it.
But that may be because we know the people and
half remember the circumstances.   If I were to
try it out on my friends they wouldn't tell me the
truth.   So I am sending you just a few pages of
the beginning.   I've not altered anything, but I've
culled it out of about three times as much.
Half my difficulty about undertaking it at all is
because in the later years what I have written
would be too revealing, and publishing it a real
cruelty to the other people involved.   Truly I'm
afraid of the later years.   They would be more
interesting than the earlier ones, but they were
written without reservations.   And they are filled
with more drama and tragedy than any one who
has known me could possibly have guessed.   Perhaps that is true of many human beings, but they
haven't spilled it all out on paper as at a confessional.
Meanwhile, perhaps there is enough human interest in these first pages to warrant my continuing to sift finely as I am doing.   I showed them to
Richard, and he says the mixture of childishness
and maturity is very confusing.   "But then," he
added, "without that touch of maturity the child
would never have written down her experiences at
all."
I have kept the occasional misspellings, but

41

there really were not many. There aren't many mistakes in grammar either, but the child had been writing for her own amusement since she was eight, and grew up in a bookish New England family. I am leaving out nothing that reflects that community and period. How extraordinary to us now, and yet how true to that day that my expectant Mother should have sent my sister and myself, children of eleven and thirteen, away from home for the entire summer, and not let us return until the new baby was two weeks old!

This is getting to be a voluminous letter, but you got me into it, didn't you? And I know of no one both experienced and honest enough to hand it to me straight.

Yours as always,
Lilla Perry

In his reply of December 5 Sandburg said, "You are in one heck of a fix. My wife and I have talked about your dilemma at great length. Your journal of your early years would make an interesting document, but a dubiously interesting book. The good passages about your later years are great, but could not be used when they name living persons. Maybe the solution would be to develop an imaginary diary, retaining all the human interest values, but altering the facts to conceal living people and places. Possibly the journal could be published fifty years from now, but to repeat, you are in one heck of a fix."

Chapter VIII

The next time I saw the Sandburgs was in the summer
of 1932. Our only communication had been a letter that I
wrote on June 1, 1930.

Dear Carl Sandburg, --
When I last set eyes on you on your last Los
Angeles visit, you were headed for Death Valley.
I wonder if you went, and what your adventure
there was. A few weeks ago we took a part of
this numerous family and went down there. Lest
you entirely forget us I am sending you an account
of our expedition. It isn't compulsory to read it,
I shan't ever know whether you do or not, but I
think you will believe that I had my yodo along with
me.
Which reminds me! I received Potato Face a
few weeks ago, with the compliments of Harcourt
and Brace. Nice of Mr. Harcourt to do that,
wasn't it? We continue to correspond at times.
My fear is that he will become quite disgusted at
the slow rate at which "the diary" progresses.
The present portion of it is still too engrossing for
me to steal away and take the necessary time to
put that earlier portion in shape. The present
chapters of it are too absorbing and interesting.
That's the whole trouble. It was awfully kind of
you to interest him in it. Is he young, middle-
aged or old? There may possibly be a book if we
live long enough, both Harcourt and I, I mean. I
am still incredibly young myself, but I don't know
a thing about him. Next time I go to New York,
next fall perhaps, would it do for me to go and
have a peep at him?

I seem to be asking you a lot of questions, but they are all rhetorical. I haven't the faintest idea that you will answer. It can't be so terribly much of an effort, however, for all the letters I've ever seen of yours read like telegrams. Never mind, the Perry family always feels a warm glow whenever we see your name in print, and even your caricature in the L. A. Times this morning was passed around with excitement. Whenever Richard has a new girl I can see him making off with your books of poems under his arm, still filled with all those little markers that stick out like sheaves. He must use them as some sort of test. Though Heaven knows why. As one of my friends said to you long ago, there isn't a single love poem among them. I think your reply was that you had had those privately printed.

Remember me to Mrs. Sandburg. Come back someday and bring her along.

Yours, as ever,
Lilla Perry

I had a three hour session a long time ago with your Lincolniana friend, Mr. Barker.

In 1932 I was traveling East with my daughter Dorothy to enter her in one of the large music conservatories. She was sure to win a scholarship at one of them.

Much had happened in our own family since I saw Sandburg last. The stock-market crash of 1929 had cleaned out all our savings. Our home was clear of any mortgage, and Everett's position, as head of the Los Angeles Public Library, was assured, so we were not as badly off as most people. The trying years since 1929, however, had undermined my husband's health. He took our own losses harder than I did, for none of the children except Richard had been put through college. The constant cutting of the salaries in the library, in which he always included his own, was a trial to him. All day his office was besieged with people seeking jobs, any kind of job in order to eat. There were nights when he paced the floor, unable to get the sorrows he had met off his mind. One day he told me that a highly equipped man with a Ph.D., and other letters after his name, had come in begging for a page's job at $60 a month, or a janitor's job, or anything at all to support his family. There was nothing for him.

44

During my visit East Mother was taking care of my household as usual, and I was proud and hopeful of what I would find for Dorothy. The invitation from the Sandburgs for us to stop on our way through Chicago had been most warm and enticing.

We had received a letter from Harbert, Michigan, written on June 14, mentioning Sandburg's preoccupation with the final revisions and illustrations for a book to be published six months thence by Harcourt. However, Dorothy and I would be welcome for a visit, whether he was there or not. Mrs. Sandburg and the girls were eager to greet us both and to hear and watch Dorothy perform on the violin. A request for confirmation of a definite date, and instructions and directions were added, as to taking a train to Michigan City and a bus from there to Harbert.

Mrs. Sandburg drove thirty-two miles to meet us at our train. I never understood why we took no bus. They had left Elmhurst and were living at Harbert in a big house overlooking the lake. There were cottages and a few houses all around them, but these were occupied only in the summertime, I gathered. All the long winter the Sandburg place was an isolated spot. Mrs. Sandburg drove the children to a school six miles away. Its isolation was ideal for the concentrated work Carl was doing on the Lincoln war years. The constant visitors at Elmhurst, so near Chicago, had been a continuous interruption. Now none but the most intimate friends ventured on this day's trip out of Chicago. For Carl it was a perfect situation for work and just what Paula wanted. It made her protection of his time and strength much easier. Since his fame she had made herself a constant buffer between him and the world of people who sought him.

I was aware, too, that with their vegetable garden and chickens they enjoyed a sort of experiment in "beating the Depression." Their wonderful table was bountifully supplied with their homegrown products. I doubt if Carl concerned himself with it much except to enjoy and approve it. He kept to a stiff routine of work. His breakfast was brought up to him. His first appearance of the day was at two in the afternoon, when the hearty big meal of the day was served. At the table and for an hour or two afterward he was the wonderful host, full of good talk and stories. At times he would try out on us something he had just written.

Had there not been visitors he might after a while

have gone back to his work. He did the revision of it in the later hours, he said. Since we were there, however, he gave generously of his time. Dorothy had brought her violin with her, of course, and it was a question which he enjoyed the most, her tremendous piano repertory or her more limited one for violin. He liked best to have her play the violin out on the open porch overlooking the lake, without accompaniment of any kind.

Dorothy had had fourteen years at the Denishawn dancing school. Her dance improvisations to recordings were the delight of the girls. All by herself she had become a proficient little tap dancer as well, though she had never had a lesson in that.

The Sandburg girls hovered around her, enjoying her gaiety and fun making and all the entertaining things she could do. It seemed to me that ideal as the Harbert home was for Carl, it was something less than ideal for those teenage girls, who must have found it more difficult to find friends and companions in these rural surroundings. They were disappointed when they learned that Dorothy and I could stay but a few days.

Margaret, the eldest of the three daughters, was now twenty-one. I remembered her well as a little girl of ten on my first visit. No one of the girls enjoyed Dorothy more. She was not as communicative as the other girls, but this could have been shyness on her part. When at the end of our stay Dorothy brought out an autograph book for the girls to sign, Margaret wrote in addition to her signature, a paragraph of such thoughtful and well-expressed appreciation of our visit I again realized what a fine mind she had.

We were packed up ready to leave. Carl and I were standing on the porch overlooking the lake, watching the girls come in from their last swim together. "When I see a girl like Dorothy," Carl said in an impressive voice, "I pray for her." It was a strange way of putting it, but I knew what he meant. "So much talent and vitality! Let life deal kindly with it, find uses for it, let it not come to nothing."

Dorothy entered the Juilliard School, and after a long visit with my sister in New York City I came back home again.

On January 14, 1933, I wrote to acknowledge the

46

receipt of Carl's last book, and to give him a little family
news:

My dear Sandburgs, --
The Mary Todd Lincoln book came, and went
the rounds of the family and even my friends before I had a single chance at it. I found it ab-
sorbingly interesting. I don't hear quite so much
about it among people who talk books as I did The
Prairie Years, but that may be because Lincoln as
a character interests more people than Mary Todd.
Many people say, "When do you suppose he is going to give us the Lincoln war years?"
I get skimpy little letters from Dorothy in New
York. She has a piano scholarship, but appears
to be having a fling at dancing and accompanying.
There is no piano concert stage to aim for these
days, and she is trying out other things, even a
trio in which she plays violin, which is aiming at
radio. So it goes. She is trying to find herself
and I am trying to leave her pretty much alone.
I stood over her for a good many years, you know,
when she was going through the discipline which
seems to be necessary for any equipment. I confess I rather envy her the tackling of the old
world, with so much within herself to offer, and
free from all entangling alliances. But the trouble
with me is that I still have all the energy of youth-
fulness and no longer its outlook. But that corrects
itself with time.
Though our household is reduced by two (Richard
away at Berkeley) the complications seem greater
than they used to be. I don't say anything to anyone around here about it, but E. R. P. seems at
times on the verge of a nervous breakdown, which
keeps us all tip-toeing softly, and is very hard on
the muscles of our legs. The whole world condition seems to weigh him down beyond smiling at
anything. It isn't our personal fortunes, for even
with savings wiped out, people on a salary are the
most fortunate these days, and I feel ourselves to
be so. He needs a house that is like a tower,
with a broad lake like an ocean to look out upon.
I often think of yours.
I found a worn copy of one of Hokusai's Mangwa
the other day, one of his sketch books. They were
printed about a hundred years ago and this one

appears to have passed through many hands. Remembering your interest in Hokusai I send it along to you.

Did I write Mrs. Sandburg after she sent the picture of the children to New York? I had not received one before, and was glad to have it. I am a bad letter writer. I either do not write at all, or I transcribe several whole chapters of life and fling you twenty pages to read. This time I have managed to be moderate.

Remember me to the three sea nymphs and the dogs, and my warmest regard goes with this to you both,

Sincerely,
Lilla Perry

On the first of March 1933 I had a phone call from Mary Lou Wenig. She was secretary of the English honorary society, Epsilon Phi, of the University of Southern California. She and two other young girls, the president of the society, Marion Darlington, and Mary Keller, the treasurer, were arranging a series of literary programs at the college. They had secured Robert Frost, Christopher Morley, T. S. Eliot, and Carl Sandburg. In their correspondence with Mr. Sandburg he had told them that when in Los Angeles he always stayed with the Perrys. Their place was like home to him. What Miss Wenig wanted to know was whether it would be all right for the three of them to bring him out to my house after they had met him at his train and taken him to lunch. I assured her that it would.

It was about three o'clock when they all arrived, the three girls, whom Carl and I always referred to afterward as the triumvirate, and Carl himself. They had been making a tour of the second-hand bookstores and been having a very gay time indeed. It was evident that the enjoyment of these three adoring girls and Carl himself had been great.

Carl's talk was given the following night, March second (it was the day F. D. R. had declared a bank holiday) and he gave them a program of the reading of his poems, some stories and the singing of some folk songs. Dr. Von Kleinsmid, the president of U.S.C., gave a reception for him afterward, but the girls got us away as soon as possible, for a buffet supper and a get-together of a few congenial people had been planned at the home of the moving-picture actress Gloria Stuart. We did not get home, I remember, until four o'clock in the morning.

Carl had been willing that I should plan an open house for my friends on the following Sunday evening. One of the girls had brought along the very elderly father of one of the older professors at the college. He had known Lincoln, and it was thought that Carl might be interested in hearing his reminiscences. They were all interesting, but one incident stood out. "Lincoln told me a story once," the old gentleman said, "but it would never do to tell it with ladies present."

"That is something easily remedied," Carl said, "Let's go for a walk around the block." Carl took hold of the old man's arm and off they went. They were not gone long but when they returned Carl had a broad grin.

I must have given Carl some current journal material to take along, for a letter of his written soon after that visit, on March 17, promised the return of my manuscripts and expressed appreciation for the opportunity to read the account of the previous visit, with its affection, heavy pigmentation, and a double portrait that was slightly unfair to us both. (He was referring to his treatment of Katherine Smith.) He liked my Death Valley sketch, which he said read like a short story. He missed seeing Laddie and Lass (probably Richard and his wife Frances) at his Mills College lecture, but they didn't show up. He hoped that "God's visitation of terror," the big Long Beach earthquake of March 10, 1933, did not even loosen one chunk of plaster.

I continued to see much of Mary Lou Wenig and Mary Keller. Marion Darlington, however, seemed to have dropped out of sight.

On May 4, 1933, Carl wrote me another letter. I do not remember what I had sent him. I suspect that it was still another account of one of his Los Angeles visits. Carl commended me for my good sportsmanship in sending along the sketch. He told of Margaret's typing a copy without any prompting, commenting to her father on how well I could write. The rest of the letter was full of Carl's usual interesting imagery.

My husband died in October of 1933. I received from Carl one of the finest letters he had ever sent me. It was such a wonderful letter that I wanted to share it with my best friend of that period of my life, Dr. Dorothea Moore. I wish I had sent a copy, for I never got the letter back. There was a time when I could have repeated it word for word. Today I remember only the beginning, "Dear Lilla, The news comes hard."

News photo of Carl Sandburg by George Watson, Los Angeles Times staff photographer, ca. 1926. From Delmar Watson Archives.

Chapter IX

The next time I heard from the Sandburgs word came that they were on their way home from a trip to Honolulu, where Carl had been giving lectures at the University of Hawaii. Their telegram from Merced gave the time of their arrival as 8:40 a.m., on April 5, 1934.

At nine in the morning as many of the family as could be assembled were at the ramp of the new Los Angeles Union Station. Fortunately it was a morning when Caswell, my second son, was not working. Dorothy, too, was at home and able to join us. We picked up Norman, my youngest boy, on the way back from the station. He had gone downtown to collect his paycheck. Since their father's death the year before both the boys had been working part-time in the library to help toward their college expenses. We laughed at Norman's request that he might this time have my bankbook and put his money in the bank himself. He apparently wanted the importance of that financial experience.

The Sandburgs were pleased at the "committee" to meet them, and we rushed them home to a breakfast of fruit, bacon and eggs, toast, and coffee.

Three Japanese sword guards on the mantel in the living room caught Carl's attention at once. Someone had given him a sword guard in Honolulu, and he was alive to them for the first time. When he learned that I had thirty more he was eager to see them all. We went upstairs to my sitting room and sat down before the chest in which I keep them. It was a joy to show them, for the Sandburgs were so appreciative of them as little masterpieces of design and craftsmanship.

51

I told Carl about my writing workshop on the third floor, and to give him an idea of the mere bulk of my effort in the last months I brought down a pile of manuscript consisting of about twelve or fourteen short stories. He ran through the titles and the beginnings.

"Don't be discouraged about rejection slips," he said. "They really mean very little as to the value of what you send out. Their reception seems to depend entirely on chance, on whether the editor is in the right mood for your particular kind of production, or whether he has material ahead. One of my early books was turned down by the first publisher to whom I sent it, and taken with enthusiasm by the second. In the game you are trying to play success is nine-tenths persistence. And you've got that, Lilla Perry."

Yes, I have, I said to myself, but I've never applied it in this direction before. Perhaps I shall be glad someday that I am driven this time. With Everett's death so soon after our losses in the Depression it was necessary that I become a money earner in some direction. The children's needs were at their peak. Only Richard was through college.

We loafed through the day in the way they wanted. Sandburg would have liked to have seen Rupert Hughes, and I suggested calling him up. But his second feeling was that with Rupert's deafness it would be slow getting into any real conversation. He would need at least three hours, and so had better not try.

He played for a little with the idea of seeing Charlie Chaplin again, and for a while we had the plan of driving out to his studio. But the purpose lagged.

Unwilling to spend time in getting lunch I left the children with Mother and took the Sandburgs up to Wilshire Boulevard. We sat in a colorful patio and ate our luncheon under trees, a long leisurely lunch with much talk. The last time I was there I had found Upton Sinclair at the next table. He had pulled me and my companion off to hear some famous psychic or medium afterward. It was in 1930 that he wrote his book about his experiments with mental telepathy, Mental Radio, published by Boni.

I told Carl a story that pleased him about the netsuke, those little masterpieces of ivory or wood carving that were used by the Japanese as a sort of toggle to suspend a tobacco

pouch or a medicine box from the belt. I had a collection
of them, and Carl never failed to ask to look them over when
he came on his visits. An English traveler had found an
Oriental busily at work on one of them. "I am going inland
for about a month," said he. "On my return I would like to
buy that netsuke of you to take back to England." "It will
be three years before this is completed," answered the Oriental.

Carl commented, "It will be two years more before
I shall begin to read proof on Lincoln: The War Years. I
have only ploughed the surface in the last two years, and I
have been working at it steadily."

Paula spoke up: "It means a lot to Carl that he does-
n't have to hold up his main project to get out a book or a
series of articles every year to keep us going. He can work
now with the perfectionist spirit in which he has always liked
to do things."

Until this visit I had always thought Paula's name was
Lilian. "It really is," she said, "but Carl changed it, and
has always called me Paula." It was Paula, too, who
changed Sandburg's name back to Carl. For a long time he
had been Charles to all his friends, and signed himself so
in the first things he published.

We discussed Mary Lou Wenig's letter to me from
New Orleans. In her adventures in the old French Quarter
she had followed around in the foot tracks she had found in
the diary pages I had given her about my own adventures
there. He had read her letter carefully. She had been one
of the three sorority girls who had called him to the coast
for a program early in 1933.

"Did you notice what the bookstore men said to her
about their dislike of Faulkner?" I asked.

"Yes, I did. I've never met him."

"I've always wished that I had never met his book
Sanctuary," added Paula. "I've read a good many things not
meant for Puritans, but nothing that ever struck me as dis-
agreeably as Sanctuary. It left images I would gladly erase
from my mind."

"I can understand his wanting to do that book," Sandburg drawled. "We've had so much sex stuff, so much

half-baked Freudian stuff that's gone over, that I can well imagine this man--who really can write--saying to himself, 'Hell! I'll shoot you one, if that is what you want!' And some of the book is great writing. Can't you just see that old man on the porch!" Sandburg painted him again for us in vivid stabbing words.

Carl read aloud the first paragraph of a highly praised novel Paula had with her. It began like a biblical story with a description of a shepherd and his sheep. "That's not good writing," he said, closing the book. "There is no smell of the sheep in it."

Somewhere during the talk he had said of his poetry, "I'm not the poet of the rose. I'm the poet of the potato plant blossom."

After we had reached the house the children had to have their innings. Dorothy had to play for them, at Carl's demand, Henry Cowell's "Tides of Maunanon." Carl's voice boomed out for us the verse that stands at the beginning. "Maunanon was the God of motion." "'God of motion' is bad," he interrupted, "The word God has been used so much that as a symbol it's meaningless." He improvised new lines. Then Dorothy played "The Tides," this powerful thing of Cowell's, suggestive of cosmic forces. It demands so much more of the piano than we usually ask that Cowell at the end had to use elbows and the full forearm, rolling along the keys, to get the effect he wanted. Dorothy did not play it as she did at Carl's house on her way to New York. Perhaps he did not know it, but I did. And she knew that I did. There has to be absolute certainty before there can be abandonment, and abandonment was not there.

Beatrice's story of one of her young friends quite convulsed us. Her school friend had expressed the belief that since the Bible did not mention dinosaurs there were no such things. "But what about the bones over in the Exposition Park Museum?" Beatrice had asked. "Yes, I know," the school chum had replied. "That's what worries me!"

Earlier in the day Norman had disappeared with his tennis racquet. I told them of his depressed mood the evening before after the final round of a tennis tournament. In it he had been nip and tuck with another boy but had made one stroke that the boys had refused to count. "I showed them this paragraph in the rules of the game which plainly shows that my stroke was right--and still the boys refused to count it! It isn't that I cared so much about winning the tournament--I won the last one--but it was the illogicalness of their decision. I can't understand minds that work that way. But there are many people, I've discovered," he added ruefully, "that don't seem to have any logic in their thinking."

"How about your own family?" I asked for fun.

"Oh this family is Heaven for logic! Whatever other faults it may have it's always strong in logic!"

A few hours later I found Norman up in his sitting room still brooding over that decision. Some illusion had been shattered; some bit of faith in human nature destroyed. I threw my arms around him (I don't very often, because boys don't like it much), and kissed him. "Strange! How I love my boys!" I exclaimed.

He looked at me with a twinkle in his eye. "'Taint logical!" he laughed.

The Sandburgs laughed when I told them the story.

"Lilla Perry is always full of such stories," Carl said. "I have always, from the first days that I began to come here, found this to be the most interesting family."

"Yes, Carl has always said so," put in Paula. "But what surprises me is the size, that there are really only four children besides your son in Washington. Carl always talked about them as if there were seven or eight at least!"

I laughed heartily. "I have heard that before. People have always seemed to have the impression that there were about fourteen! Sometimes the five have seemed like fourteen!"

Before they left Sandburg asked me to let him have some of the last few things I have done in my writing. I picked out two of the last stories and he put them in his bag. "I've always believed you could write, you know," he commented. "I'll read every word of these."

Dorothy and Beatrice drove with us to the station, and the last ten minutes at the train were spent in listening to Sandburg's amusing imitation of the Chinese restaurateur in Honolulu who had introduced him at an Oriental banquet as "The Melican Li Po."

Chapter X

In 1935 I made another visit to the Sandburg home on Lake Michigan. On June 16 I sent off the following letter:

My dear Sandburgs--

July 12th Caswell and I are starting in our car for a trip across the continent. He says we shall be in Chicago on the 16th. We are visiting friends there for a few days at 1205 N. State Street, and shall be in Hinsdale for a day also. It will be quite irresistible not to drive to Harbert to have a look-in upon you. Perhaps it is on our way toward New York. My geographical sense isn't strong so I can't say. Not having Dorothy with us this time to play piano, violin or clog, I have dusted off the Cuban dances which you used to call for years ago. Someone has made off with our record of your Negro spirituals and Boll Weevil. I have regretted it very much, but I fear it would be almost more than I could stand to listen to it yet--Everett used to ask so often for us to play that record, even during his illness. What is it that happens in the passage of years that makes me know that someday I shall be able to listen to those old tunes without tears? But not yet.

I have had a busy year of teaching. I am looking to this trip and to seeing my old friends more than I can express even though they will have to be "touch and go" visits, since on account of Caswell's work and my own, we have to be back in California in six weeks.

Here's hoping that I may have a word that we shall find you at home on that lookout over Lake Michigan.

Yours as always,
Lilla Perry

P.S. I judge the Lola Journal was just--unspeaka-
ble! And the less said about it the better. Apparently Sidney Sanders is still continuing his efforts
to place it. I shall try to see him while in New
York City.

We knew that we would be welcome, for back on February 13 Carl had enjoined me to consider his home as a
stop on the underground railroad when I began my cross-
country trip. He had asked me to tell Gordon Ray Young
that he appreciated both the Civil War material that he had
received from him and his faith that he could take Lincoln
through the storm. He had promised that upon my arrival
there would be reports on humans, our feathered friends,
and the insects. Our bugs, he had said, possessed many
highly developed characteristics, and we would discuss my
journal, which should not be deficient in insect qualities.
He had wished me a pleasant trip.

This letter in my files is only a copy of the one received. The original I sent to Gordon Ray Young. Mr.
Young was for a long time a book reviewer on the staff of
the L.A. Times and a novelist himself. I thought it might
help heal his hurt at never having had any acknowledgement
of the pile of Civil War material he had sent to Carl. He
had collected it for a book of his own.

It was during this visit that I became well acquainted
with Carl's own special quarters on the third floor of his
house. It was, indeed, a workshop. It overflowed with
books, housed for the most part in apple boxes or orange
crates turned on their sides. There was a large sun deck
and I recall sitting there one afternoon with the family,
watching a terrific storm gather over the lake.

The guest room in which I slept was called the Lincoln room. Three walls were completely lined, from floor
to ceiling, with the library of books on Lincoln. I was impressed with the quantity of Congressional and other govern-
mental reports, many of them with paper markers still left
between the leaves.

Carl's next visit to me must have been on January 6,
1937, for I find a telegram from him in my files with the

previous day's date, saying that he would arrive on Wednesday morning at ten-thirty, on the Santa Fe, posing the usual questions and felicitations.

I find no account of that 1937 visit. He was in town for a speaking engagement at Pomona College on Thursday, the 7th, and his stay lasted but a few days. For myself, I was deep in the problems of earning a living and putting my children through college. To accomplish this through writing--as I would have preferred to do--seemed to require too long and precarious an apprenticeship. I had turned to the immediately remunerative field of piano teaching. I had once taught in a small conservatory in New York City. I had taught all of my own children to play. My equipment was good and my success almost immediate. My clientele was mainly the children of the motion-picture stars. In the lean interval of getting started I had rented to congenial "paying guests" every available portion of my large house not utilized by my own family. It enabled me to keep free of cooking and housework, which I had seldom done. But I did all the marketing and the menu planning. This, with the general supervision of the housework and my teaching (at the pupils' own homes) made me a more than busy person. It is little wonder that I find no written account of Carl's visit in 1937. I found no time to do it. There is nothing left except his telegram to tell me that he was here.

One of the episodes of that visit I do remember, however, though I never wrote it down. Carl wanted to cash an eight-hundred-dollar check that he had received for a program. "Where is your bank?" he asked me. I told where it was, quite near, up on Wilshire Boulevard. He returned after a little with a broad grin. "They didn't know me," he laughed, "so they wouldn't cash it."

Mr. Judson D. Metzgar overheard the conversation. "Come on down to my bank. They will cash it for you there." Mr. Metzgar was a very dear friend now living with us. He was probably the best expert in America on Japanese prints. This mutual interest had probably formed the basis of our long friendship.

Off they went. Sandburg sat down and waited while Mr. Metzgar took the check up to his cashier's window. He always made friends with anyone who served him, and he had often had friendly talks with the girl cashier.

"I want you to cash a check for a friend of mine. It is Carl Sandburg, so you would know who he is anyway."

"Should I know?" she asked.

"Why, of course. Any man on the street knows who Carl Sandburg is. I'll prove it. I'll ask the man back of me in this line."

He turned to the man back of him. "This young lady doesn't know who Carl Sandburg is. Can you tell her?"

"Why, yes," the man said, "Carl Sandburg has written the greatest life of Lincoln ever written, and by many people is considered to be America's greatest free-verse poet."

"What did I tell you?" Mr. Metzgar said to her.

The check was cashed, of course.

These were the years when Carl was deep in the research and the writing of the Lincoln War Years. He once told me that the project took him ten years.

There was another visit by Carl that was not noted or recorded in my journal, in March 1938, but referred to in this letter I wrote on March 20, 1938:

> Dear Carl:
> What a terrible way to get you to the station! And I should be ashamed to tell you what was the matter with my car! Merely out of gas. And I never do such a thing!
> I know you arrived at the train and at your destination, however, for I got glowing accounts of your Mills program from Mary Lou. In fact she spills over so much that I won't enclose her letter lest it hopelessly spoil you. On glancing it over, however, I find so much to amuse me that would amuse Mrs. Sandburg also that I have decided to enclose it after all, and send all of this on to her. Maybe you won't ever see it but I will give her the fun of reading it.
> The records have just arrived, and threaten to be worn out by Beatrice and Norman. I do think you did yourself proud in them, and like them exceedingly. Many many thanks.

59

Helga may get a letter from Beatrice before long. She still looks upon Helga as a sort of double. Anyway, they are both two fine girls!

This is about enuf from me this time. Maybe next time you come you will drive up to the top of the high hill where Gordon Ray Young lives, and he will be glad indeed to see us. My mistake was in not pulling down shades (I never do) and he saw what he thought was a party going on.

> Yours as always, and my very best
> wishes to all of the Sandburgs,
> Lilla Perry

P.S. In my many yarns about Norman I forgot to mention that he is ping-pong and tennis champion of Cal Tech.

To this Carl replied on April 15, saying that he enclosed two letters from the bright girls we had both met on the day F. D. R. closed the banks. He had had some thoughts of keeping Mary Lou's letter against a day when the blues were hurtful. He was keeping the Gordon Ray Young letter; let him know that a visit would still transpire, and the tie that they both had been boxcar tramps still held. I should let Mr. Metzgar know that there was a Hokusai poem in Smoke and Steel. Also that he was grateful for and accepted the Japanese name he had given him and would learn to say and write it (Mr. Metzgar had written Carl in February, addressing him as "Dear Katsushika. " Katsushika was Hokusai's first name.) He felt completely submerged under the Lincoln job but had great hopes of completing it without neglecting any details by the next winter. Norman was utter genius: he felt convinced of that more than ever; he was going to pray on the sidelines. Norman's mind was exceptional. Carl's esteem for it was all the stronger because Norman worked in areas where Carl was without feet while Norman was flying. He had not yet forgotten all the strong impressions of the last visit, the rotunda [probably the program for children that Sandburg put on in the rotunda of the main library in Los Angeles one Sunday during his visit], the Perry house, the Paramount lot, etc. Blessings on the Perry household.

There were no visits back and forth for the next four years, and correspondence was sparse during this period. I wrote Carl on November 25, 1939, in connection with the long-awaited publication of the War Years:

My dear Sandburgs, --

How do you flourish? How does the Chikaming Goat Farm flourish?

Hurrah that the books are out! The baby is born at last! I can well imagine the family rejoicing that the biggest task you have ever undertaken is completed.

My four beautiful volumes arrived yesterday, and I took volume I to bed with me last night. Read straight through to page 85, to "Peace Efforts Fail." Today Bea has been busy with the fourth volume and her comment is that it is "like poetry."

It may not be very long before your publishers send you forth from your long hiding to show yourself on the lecture platform again. And in that case we at 720 Kingsley Drive will be seeing you again. I hope so. And if Mrs. Sandburg comes that will be better yet. Meanwhile, thanks indeed for your generous gift of the books.

Enthusiastically yours,
Lilla Perry

More anon about the War Years. I see I have my winter's reading cut out for me.

This letter was followed up with another on December 4, commenting on the public reception accorded the War Years.

Dear Carl Sandburg, --

This L.A. Times review might not come your way, so I am sending it on. I am certainly delighted with your generous gift to me. We were all amused at your Chikaming Goat Farm address after your signature to the foreword. "That's great!" said Norman. "That's the necessary democratic touch which shows him to be akin to the man he writes about!"

In Dawson's on Wednesday they told me their deluxe copies are sold and they believe the books are going to be a big success. After the work you put in on them you don't need anybody's say-so. But I want them to get all the laudation they deserve and be a "best-seller" as well! Have written Caswell to send me the reviews.

Yours enthusiastically,
Lilla Perry

There was another visit by Carl in January 1942, but again I kept no record of it. However, I do have a clipping from the Los Angeles Daily News for January 24, and a picture of Carl being interviewed by a group of Los Angeles reporters on my front lawn. Carl arrived on Friday, January 23, according to the Daily News article, to fill two engagements on a coast-to-coast lecture tour. His first date was at Los Angeles City College on Friday evening, and his second was at the Philharmonic Auditorium on Monday evening, so his visit with me was probably circumscribed by those two dates. The news conference on my front lawn took place on Saturday, and I received some publicity as Sandburg's hostess "off and on for the last 20 years." I have no recollection of who it was that took the snapshot, but it was not I, for I am in back of the group of reporters, while up front is Jake Zeitlin.

I did not write Carl again until May 30, 1942:

Dear Carl Sandburg, --
Every time you have thought of me since your visit here you have sent me something, first the records of The People, Yes, then the book to replace my hard worn copy, then the beautiful blue first edition! And I haven't written--perhaps for two reasons. One because for more weeks than I like to remember I have been trying to shake off a flu bug that has gotten me down. I have managed to plod along through the day's work, but haven't had an ounce of energy to spare. My second reason is that I was so sure of being forgiven. And I have just discovered a third. When I did write I wanted it to be a real letter, with something of all the things I would like to say put in. But this won't be. I am still overcome with a laziness that makes me want to do nothing on this holiday but lie down with a book. Yet I ought to be drawn to the typewriter and punching out your name for the girls have just put your record on the victrola and we have all once more been listening to your record. It has been like having you talk to us, and I am impressed more than ever with the wonderful things you do with your voice, the inflections on a single word. You have done something fine in those recordings, and I am awful glad to have them.
Sometime this week you are going to receive through the mail the first volume of the Lincoln

books from a friend of mine, Dr. Gerson. He asked me if I thought you would be willing to autograph it for him, and expressed his reluctance to burden you or someone of your household with the task of rewrapping and mailing the volume. I assured him that I would write and ask you to, and if you knew the man, the fine liberal spirit that he is, and his enthusiasm for your Lincoln, I know that you would grant his request. He is the president of the Severance Club, a group of liberally inclined people who meet for dinner, a talk by some worthwhile speaker and a discussion afterward, twice a month. He had the Lincoln books most ably reviewed at one of the sessions soon after they appeared. He was a great friend of Lincoln Steffens, which says something for him, too.

There are changes since you were here. Grandma and my sister have gone East. Mother, who is 82, had an idea that she wanted once more to revisit her New England home, and then on her return to settle down without thought of further travels. Norman is teaching Mathematics and Physics in the Santa Ana Aircraft replacement and training center. He comes in weekends and we hardly know him in a uniform which has to be kept just so. He tells us the men are criticized if they fail to button the rear pocket of their trousers! And he is shaved and has his hair trimmed. It took the army to do it. Nothing else ever could. It worried me that he always wanted to be a teacher. Now possibly he may make it.

Caswell, out here from New York on his vacation, has been seized upon by a defense job, has asked for leave of absence from the New York Library and may be out here for the duration. I see little of Richard. None of them are on the firing lines yet. But who knows before we are through.

This will just about do for this time. I should have written Mrs. Sandburg and told her that we saw more of you on this last visit than we had on many a previous one, and the memory of it is one of the pleasantest.

> With my best wishes to you both, always,
> Lilla Perry

There was some snag about getting Dr. Gerson's Lincoln volume back to him. Paula Sandburg wrote on December 16, 1942, to inquire if it had been received, and offered to make a search, disclaiming any problem with the mailing. Another note from her on January 8, 1943, indicated that it had been located and was on its way.

Press conference with Los Angeles reporters on front lawn, 720 South Kingsley Drive, Los Angeles, January 24, 1942

Chapter XI

It was in the fall of '43 that Sandburg was with us for the longest stay he ever made. He was with us for well over a month. I did not even know he was in town when he called me up from the Casa Del Mar in Santa Monica.

"Lilla, M.G.M. has asked me to come out here to write a novel which they want to put into a movie. I am to meet with them daily till we get the general skeleton worked out. But they've put me up here at this Casa Del Mar at the studio's expense, and I find I can't write a word. Isn't there a corner for me at your house, Lilla? I've been here three days now in all this elegance and I can't do a lick of work here. I've stared at the walls, unable to get a line on paper. I've always been able to work at your house. Can't you find a spot for me?"

My house was filled with people who were permanent paying guests. Among them was my sister Alice, who had come West with two daughters soon after her husband's death. She had joined me to be with Mother.

I didn't know where I could put Carl, nor even if he would like it as he had when there had been only the family. I told him to come on in town, however, and look us over.

Mother and I at the time were using two large rooms on the third floor, once called the attic. Carl had always been put into the best rooms in the house. I could easily get Mother to give up her third-floor room and take one of the twin beds in my room, but I wasn't sure Carl would like her room.

When I took him up to it he was exclamatory. With

the big sundeck leading out of it, it seemed to almost duplicate the working quarters of his place on Lake Michigan.
He was sure he could work there. He could see it was practically soundproof. He could type, if he felt like it, till
three o'clock in the morning and disturb no one. Further-
more, none of the early-morning noises, so annoying at the
hotel, would reach him. So it was decided. An M. G. M.
limousine brought him, his one bag, and a stuffed briefcase
to us the next day. As a joke and to make his workroom
look really homelike I ranged two empty apple boxes against
the wall for books. He laughed about it. But he used them!

I missed most of our eleven o'clock breakfasts. At
that hour, four mornings a week, I was out in Brentwood
teaching the Margaret Sullavan - Leland Hayward children.
Our long conversations on this visit took place in the hall of
the third floor beside my big rolltop desk, which had become
my working spot during these years. When he came in too
late for me I left notes on the corner of the desk. When he
knew I would be off in the morning too early for him he left
notes for me.

He explained why M. G. M. had summoned him to the
Coast. The original idea had been for him to write a "Cavalcade of American History" not unlike Noel Coward's Cavalcade, which had been made into a movie. As in Cavalcade
there was to be a fictional element in this, with the same
two characters reincarnated in each historical period. Carl's
ability as a writer of fiction was untested. They were virtually buying the drawing power of his name for the hundred
thousand dollars named in the contract.

Carl was entering into this project with tremendous
zest and interest. Every day about one o'clock a studio limousine called for him and took him off for conferences over
the book. He seemed to enjoy the men he worked with thoroughly. I heard many tales of Voldemar Vetluigin and Sidney Franklin. His typewriter was busy long into the night.
Often he did not return until late, but there were many times
when he joined us at dinner and entered fully into the gaiety
of it.

Often I found on the corner of my desk in the upper
hall a new or a revised chapter of the book, which afterward
became Remembrance Rock. The carbons of those first versions of the early chapters were given to me when he left.
Once he left on the old desk a sheaf of unpublished poems

66

that he was carrying around with him, retouching, refinishing. I still have the note he left with them, saying that they were segments which also came out of tumult.

He may have been referring to a tumult of my own that I had shared with him to gain help from his judgment. I had left on the desk for him a difficult letter I had felt I must write. He replied that it must have been a hard day's work to write such a letter, but that as a declaration and a prediction it would endure. It might have little influence, but I might be able to confirm the doubts I felt and besides, Sunday was a fine day to crystalize my thoughts on justice. He still had many things to tell me about. He felt that the house had a fine heritage for him and I showed him a kindness stemming from the earlier years.

Once I found on the desk thirty-eight definitions of poetry, which he called "Experimental Statements." There were corrections and changes, things he would keep on revising for a long time to come.

It hardly seems possible that I did not get onto paper a fuller account of those rich days. Only certain fragments of conversation are remembered. He told me of Helga's marriage, a runaway marriage really. Helga must have known that the boy was not the type her parents would have chosen to have her marry.

One breakfast time at eleven, when I chanced to be home, Emil Ludwig came to the door. Coming unannounced as he did, I supposed he had an appointment with Sandburg, and brought him to the dining table, where we were having coffee. Sandburg was cool in his greeting, I thought. I did not know that Ludwig and all his methods in biography and history were anathema to Carl. It was evident during the interview that Ludwig was trying to get biographical material for a sketch of Sandburg, and Carl would contribute nothing.

"Why don't you do Einstein? You know Einstein."

"Yes, of course I know Einstein," said Ludwig. "But Einstein and I, we mix like oil and water. I cannot do Einstein."

Before Ludwig left Sandburg heard him inviting me to his open house, Sunday afternoons. "Don't you go," Carl said, as we stood watching our departing visitor get into his car. "He wants you to come because he thinks he can get material from you that I will not give him. I don't like his methods. He is no honest researcher. He tells you what Napoleon thought, as if he could possibly know. Did you hear what he said about Einstein--that he and Einstein mix like oil and water! Why, it is as if the midge, born in the morning and dying at evening, were to say of itself and an eagle--we!"

That, as he himself would have said, was a good line. I have heard him get off many a good line that I have lost because there was no time to take it down.

I have heard the story of the young playwright who took Sandburg to a performance of one of his plays to get his opinion of it. He was angry because Sandburg slept through the play. When the playwright berated him, his answer seems just like him. "Young man," said Carl, "Sleep is an opinion!" Since then I have heard this same reply attributed to Winston Churchill, but it sounded so exactly like Carl that I have never doubted it.

One morning Will Rogers Jr. came to the door. Carl had not yet come downstairs. As we sat talking together I think I surprised the young man by saying suddenly, "I believe I can guess why you have come to see Carl Sandburg!" When I explained that I surmised it was to get Carl to write a life of his father, he admitted that I was right. Every one in his family felt that Sandburg was the man to do it. His mother was ready to turn over to him everything she had in the way of material that would be a help.

The talk with Sandburg later was inconclusive. Carl admitted that he had too much ahead of him to which he was committed, and the life of Will Rogers ought not to wait until he could undertake it.

We sat long at the table over coffee, and I heard many tales from both men rich in interest about Will Rogers. Carl, too, had known him and had his stories to tell. His son told us that there was never an old cowboy who turned up at the ranch whom his father didn't come forth to meet and swap roping tricks with. He remembered how in the New Years Eve flood of 1934 the bridge near their ranch had been weakened and nearly washed away. He and his brother were coming home from some late party. As they came to the bridge they found an old man in high boots and raincoat swinging a lantern and warning people away from it. To their surprise they found it was their Dad, and he had been out there all night.

Although Carl never met Dr. James T. Fisher, it was while he was at the house this time that I was occasionally going out to dinner, or to a movie, with Dr. Fisher. He was Everett's old golfing pal. We had a good cook, and once in a while I would invite him to have dinner with us at the house. He was a great talker and everyone seemed to find him very amusing. I did, too, to a certain extent, but I knew that Dr. Fisher wanted to marry me, and that made our relationship a trifle difficult. I had not the slightest idea of marrying again. He was in his seventies, and his notion was not to be taken too seriously. I played along and continued to go out with him, mainly--I have to confess it-- because he was my only source for getting gas coupons. Without them I could not have carried on my music teaching.

The war was on. We were strictly rationed on gas for our automobiles, and though I had gone to my gas-rationing board and pleaded with tears in my eyes, explaining that my livelihood and that of my children still in school depended on my getting about in my car, I couldn't get one gallon allowed beyond the minimum that any woman might have had for getting to the store and to the dentist. Dr. Fisher, as a physician, could get all the coupons he wanted. In fact, they were issued to him in quantity. Being resident physician at a sanitarium he hardly needed any. He knew my need of them and kept me supplied. But he doled them out, just enough to keep me going or, as Mother laughingly pointed out, just enough to make sure that I did not turn him down for a next engagement. It was literally true that my living depended on those gas tickets. So I had to use diplomacy and finesse to keep Dr. Fisher interested, and gentleness and levity to parry his more serious purpose.

One morning Carl paused at my desk to find me laboring over a letter, and when I read it aloud to him he went into guffaws of laughter. He demanded a copy of it so that he might read it--for some reason--to his brother-in-law, Edward Steichen.

> Dear Dr. Fisher, --
> I am surprised at you! I had thought that having reached your sixtieth [I flattered him, for he was in his 70s] year you had attained wisdom! Here

you are "sitting pretty" on the top of the world, with an excellent salary, nurses dancing attendance at your slightest word ("Yes, Dr. Fisher. Certainly, Dr. Fisher," I hear them say), a dog at your feet, and at a crook of your little finger able to summon as friend and companion, and for as brief a time as need be, any one you desire to share a dinner or a dance, a film or a frolic. And with all this--you stick out your neck for trouble!

Beautifully free of all entangling alliances (and like all of us your life has been full of them), you begin to feel irked that you have no chafing collar around your neck, and want once more to feel the tug of a leash! Don't you know when you are well off? Gosh, I do, and I haven't yet reached your state of blessed irresponsibility. But I intend to eventually and to stay there! Take my advice and stay right there yourself.

The new cook is hopeless and I am gathering my strength to try for another. So I won't ask you to dinner this week. But try us a week from Friday. Recover your sanity and come over in a proper state of mind. You're too good company to lose, and we'd miss you.

Yours, as always,
L. P.

Intermittently, because he was always darting off to Mexico or South America or somewhere, I saw Dr. Fisher up to the time of his death in 1950. He never gave up his little idea, but he was always good fun. The year preceding his death he published a book that for many months was on the best-seller list. It was called A Few Buttons Missing; The Case History of a Psychiatrist. I had heard many of the stories in it, but I had forgotten that he had studied with Freud and that his training in psychiatry had been so extensive. Long afterward Carl Sandburg had a look at the book and remarked to me with a laugh, "Maybe we underestimated him, Lilla." Perhaps we did, but it wouldn't have mattered.

It was during this 1943 visit of Carl's that we had the Birdwell family with us. I had put my usual advertisement for domestic help in the paper, reading "Room and board to couple plus $50 a month in exchange for wife's work." Fifty dollars was low at the time. The bait was the living expenses for the two, which were heavy. I always got wonderful answers to this ad, and at a time when my friends, paying top wages, were not able to get any domestic help at all. Defense work had drawn them off.

It was Birdwell himself who made the deal with me to take in his two boys, twelve and fourteen, instead of paying the $50 cash. There was an unused play room out in the garage that could be heated, and I fixed it up for the boys. Birdwell himself was a fine-looking, suave individual. Carl said of him, "If he were to appear on a movie lot they would cast him for a senator." His wife was a very pretty Irish woman, and a good but reluctant cook. She had no wish to support the entire family by her labors, and Birdwell's promises of being a great help to her in the intervals between hunting a job were just promises, and nothing more. She got a great deal of help from the boys, however. Boys of their age might easily have been a nuisance in any strange household, but they were models of behavior. I never even felt a complaint about them. Their mother insisted that they do the waiting on table, and after I instructed them how I wanted it done, they did it excellently. The younger one, Warren, had once had piano lessons and showed considerable interest in learning to play. So I gave him piano lessons regularly. On Saturdays, when he was not in school, I drove him around to music lessons with me. If I left him in the car, the Leland Hayward children would go out and get him, and seemed always to find him a wonderful pal. Tarquin Olivier, Laurence Olivier's young son, was always full of regrets if I had failed to bring Warren along with me. I would leave him to play with Tarquin while I went nearby to give Barbara Hutton's son, Lance Reventlow, his music lesson. I never saw any need for Warren's father or mother to exercise the least discipline in the bringing up of those two boys. They were just naturally obedient and naturally endowed with good manners. Thinking of my own obstreperous three boys, I used to look at them and marvel!

One night at dinner Carl was holding forth with one of his very best stories. Warren alone was clearing the table at the time. He had brought in the last serving of dessert. He could think of nothing that would give him further excuse for lingering in the dining room. Carl saw his predicament and purposely dragged out his story. Warren saw some imaginary crumbs at the edge of the rug. He stooped and picked them up with deliberation. Then a spot on the polished floor caught his attention. With a paper napkin he scrubbed and he scrubbed. Those of us at the table who were onto his actions were convulsed. It was not until Carl reached the point of his tale that Warren's concern with further spots on that floor was relieved.

There had been much publicity in the paper about Carl's program at the Philharmonic, and it was known that an M. G. M. limousine called for him every day at one o'clock and took him to the studio. The Birdwells were quite impressed with the celebrity of our houseguest. However, Carl's visit this time was long. Though Mother or myself always attended to his eleven o'clock breakfast, there may have been other irregularities where we didn't take up the slack that had proved irksome to temperamental "help." At any rate, Carl told the following story with hoots of laughter. He was sitting looking over his mail at a late breakfast one morning when the phone rang in the music room. There was no one around to answer it at the moment and Carl let it ring, of course. It must have continued ringing for some time, for at length "the senator" burst in from the kitchen and answered it himself. He had to stride through the dining room and it didn't help in the least that it proved to be "wrong number." As he passed through the dining room again he paused by the table a minute and looked at Sandburg. "Let a phone ring like that, and not stir!" he muttered. Then more fiercely he added, "You're not as important as you think you are!" Carl told and retold that story with booming laughter.

It was on account of this tale (because the Birdwell family were characters right out of a book to Carl, anyway) that I afterward wrote Carl what happened when we took them to my recital in Brentwood at Joan Crawford's. When the Birdwells joined us in the automobile to be taken along to the program I was aware that no motion-picture stars in my audience would have anything on that couple for looks. Maybe their clothes weren't expensive, but they wore them with an air that would have deceived anyone. Warren was on my program, of course, and he played a Tony Martin arrangement of a Tschaikowski concerto with such swaying enjoyment of the rhythm that it made the listeners in his audience look at each other and smile.

After the program was over I saw "the senator" stride up to Gary Cooper as he was passing through a doorway, hold out his hand and say, "I'm Granville Birdwell. Pleased to meet you, Mr. Cooper." Gary Cooper shook the hand held out to him with a slightly puzzled frown on his face. "I'm sure I <u>ought</u> to know who you are," he was doubtless thinking.

On the ride home "the senator" described to his wife and the rest of us his introduction to Gary Cooper. "After all, I'm one of his public. I'm one of the people who put him where he is today!"

Birdwell had been on the police force up in San Francisco, so he told me. I came at last to have as little faith in his efforts to get a job in Los Angeles as did his wife. In her exasperation at being the entire support of the family, with what money the two boys with their paper route and other jobs could bring in, her Irish temper exploded one day. It hit not only her husband, but me, as well. And the Birdwells left. I was sorry to see the last of those fine boys.

One night coming home a little earlier than usual Sandburg found me at my big hall desk absorbed in the reading of some letters. My niece Carol, who worked at Red Cross, had brought them to me. They were the letters of a naval officer in action in the Pacific, a man named Kenneth Dodson--written to his wife. His wife had given them to his sister to read and his sister, also at Red Cross, had given them to Carol.

"Carl," I exclaimed, "these are wonderful letters! The man is over there now, going through all this. These are letters home to his wife. And written--well, you'll see. Let me read you some of this."

Carl sat down at the end of the desk and listened, as only Carl Sandburg could listen.

I began to read just where I had left off:

> One night I worked with my boys until midnight transferring 62 wounded men to a hospital ship. Some groaned, some talked out of their head. One poor kid screamed through grit teeth from the pain of moving his terrible bone fractures. We worked as gently as we could. One fine looking tall boy extended over both ends of his stretcher. He was shot through the leg and the bone was shattered. For some reason I was impelled to ask him where he was from. He said, "South East Oregon" and mentioned a small town near Ashland. I told him

73

my brother-in-law had a fox farm at Eagle Point. We were just picking him up to put him in the boat and he smiled in the moonlight and said, "Eagle Point fox farm. I know him. He sure has beautiful foxes!" He gripped my hand hard. Then we picked up his litter and lowered it into the boat to start him on his way home. Well, I'd got through all the groaning and the boy who couldn't help screaming through his grit teeth, and I'd kept a stiff upper lip, but as that smiling kid left I had to rub away the tears with my fist. I hate war.

War leaves a stamp on you. You take a bath and don't feel clean. You want a spiritual purge of the whole stinking business. You feel like you'd like to be baptised and have communion. You want to lie on the grass on a windy hill in the summertime and smell the clean drying grasses and watch the cumulus swimming by in the blue of the sky. You want to have your arms around one very near and dear to you and snuggle your head deep beside your loved one and feel the tenderness of her lips on yours and the clean warm living scent that is her. Then sleep. And there shall be no more war, no parting, no killing, no smell of death. Just peace.

I had had difficulty getting through that last paragraph. I looked up at Carl and his face showed all that I had been feeling.

He took the sheaf of letters from my hand. "May I have these for a while? I want to get in touch with that man. He has a gift of expression there that must not be wasted." Did I know who the man was, where he was now, where he could be reached? I didn't, but I could easily find out through Carol, who had brought me the letters.

This was the beginning. Carl never let up in his interest in Kenneth Dodson. Of course he was a writer, at least, a man who wanted to write. Carl gave him every encouragement.

Chapter XII

After the long visit of August-September 1943 there was again a considerable interval before Carl came out to work at M.G.M. Studio, broken only by one quick visit on September 17, 1944. There was a succession of letters and telegrams from him in 1944, 1945, and 1946, explaining the delays and postponements, mostly because his contact man, Sidney Franklin, was tied up with other studio projects, or on vacation.

In a telegram of January 18, 1944, he expected to be delayed until March; this was soon postponed to June 1. A telegram of July 7 announced further postponement, soon confirmed by letter as being September 15. This proved to be the flying visit of September 17, duly confirmed by a telegram from Albuquerque on the 16th, signed Carlos Sandoza. On November 15 he merely reported progress on the writing project. In February 1945 he talked of sending M.G.M. some two hundred and sixty pages, but he didn't expect to see them until April in Los Angeles. A note of August 1945 gave statistics on the script: a 12,000-word prologue, 188,000 words in Book I, an estimated 100,000 in Book II, with perhaps another 100,000 in Book III and the Epilogue. It then looked like September or October before he would be out, he said. Again in November he wrote that it would be late November or December. And so it went.

It was a period, however, when I could not have complained of Carl's failure to write; we exchanged numerous letters. In addition, I seemed to receive more books than ever. In April 1944, for example, he shipped me two packages of books. On October 2, 1943, in reply to his request for information about songs at the time of the Puritans, I sent him the following:

Dear Carl, --

A few minutes ago I called up my old friend, Sam Kreider, and asked him if he knew what songs the Puritans were singing at the time they landed in this country. He is left so high and dry and alone in his hobby of collecting the popular songs of all eras that he went into an outburst which must have lasted twenty minutes. He has twenty or thirty he tells me that he can authenticate. One of the oldest tunes, he tells me, is the one we now sing to the words, "For he's a jolly good fellow." It is an old tune of the crusades, sung then to words something like "We're on our way to Jerusalem." It was later a French popular song deriding Marlborough, "Malbruck ne va en guerre" (will not go to war). He believes the words the Puritans used for it can be found. The movies, I thought, call on him occasionally for information when they are stuck for a song of some particular era. Perhaps they have done so five times in five years, he laughed. But nobody but myself seems to know how deeply he has gone into this hobby of his, and how far back he has dug. When you come back I want you to meet him. I feel sure you will find him rich in material if you want to use musical background of the periods you are dealing with. He always makes me want to throw overboard all my other hobbies and join him in his, he makes it so fascinating. I am afraid his wife, whom I have known, too, for years, resents his music collecting and his enthusiasms because he has never tried and I think never cared to make it remunerative.

> So much for this time,
> Lilla

On the 7th of November I wrote Carl, acknowledging the gift of John Sanford's The People from Heaven, which Harcourt had just published, and which Catherine McCarthy, Sandburg's editor, had written me about, enclosing Carl's review of the Sanford book.

In early 1946 Carl's life was further complicated by the Sandburg family's move to Connemara Farm, near Flat Rock, North Carolina. In a letter of January 22 I had asked him to write a letter on Norman's behalf to the National Research Council, in connection with a scholarship application.

In his reply of February 27 Carl apologized for missing the deadline on the letter for Norman, and thought that his next trip to Los Angeles would be May or June.

Later on in the spring of 1946, on June 8, I had to write a sad letter to Carl.

The Lodge
Lake Arrowhead, Calif.

Dear Carl, --
We lost little Mother on May 11th. Remembering how life seemed to center round her here at 720 you will understand what a loss she has been. Up to her last illness she had seemed well and active, a marvel for her 85 years. Every time a note from you announced a new date of arrival here her remarks would indicate her expectation of looking after your breakfasts as she always did with such pleasure.

We have taken it hard, in spite of the philosophy she tried to arm us with. My sister and I should have gotten away at once but we couldn't manage it until this last week. I kept on doggedly at my teaching till I ran into another car and pretty well smashed up my own. We are hoping a lot from this complete change and rest at Arrowhead.

As always
Lilla

I wrote again, but in a much lighter vein this time, on October 25.

Dear Carl, --
Is my face red!
Have just tackled our third floor for a housecleaning after neglect of several months, and discovered that the moths have captured your grey trousers left in my care. They have gone for all the strategic places. They wouldn't be decent enough now to feed goats. (Not that I believe that you ever feed goats.) I am so sorry and ashamed. We used to boast, in Grandma's day, that nothing at 720 had ever been lost to a moth.

You see I am writing my confession because I don't want to have to face you with the fact. We do face you again some day, don't we?

Yours, contritely, and devotedly (though not devotedly enough seemingly to keep moths out of your pants),

Lilla

Carl was still so preoccupied with the M. G. M. project that I did not hear from him until after the second letter. In his note of October 28 he admitted he was subject to reproach for not writing. But his writing job had "effloresced" beyond any size anticipated. He expected to get West the next winter. He regarded the loss of Gram as a personal thing and would miss her. Always good to him, she was a sturdy, fine woman, of the pioneer stock. He expected that we would have an unlimited exchange of news. In a postscript he said he had received the bulletin about the vandal moths, which he regarded as the least of our troubles.

It is just as well that Carl's prediction as to his coming West "the next winter" was as far off as some of his earlier calculations. About nine months later he heard of my cancer operation through Mary Keller, and sent me a telegram on August 1, 1947, offering his prayers for my recovery and an improvement to the point that I could play all of Bach. I replied as follows, as of August 8:

Dear Carl, --
Thanks for that kind wire after you got the news about me from Mary Keller!

I took that particular trip to hell and back again last November, but if you should arrive today you would never know that I had been away. Perhaps I wouldn't even tell you!

Doctor and surgeon tell me that I got to them in time. I hope so. Convalescence, however, was slow, took about five months, and there was a time when I was certainly afraid that the dog was going to snap up my chocolate frosting! Do you remember the story?

A man who was trying to decide how he should leave his property to his three sons sat watching them eat large slices of chocolate cake. The oldest ate off all the chocolate frosting first, but when he got to the cake part it tasted dry and not sweet enough, so he threw it away. The second son carefully removed the chocolate and set it aside to be eaten last, but while he was munching the cake, a

78

dog came along and snapped up the frosting. Meanwhile the youngest son sat nibbling alternately on the cake and the chocolate, and he ate it all. "That boy will always be able to take care of himself, " decided the father. "I'll divide my property between the two oldest, who will need it. "

I'm nibbling on both cake and chocolate nowadays. Please come out soon and add to the frosting in my life!

Yours, affectionately,
Lilla

By the spring of 1948 I was feeling well enough to think of traveling again, and arranged to coincide with another transcontinental trip of Caswell's in July, so that he could drive me East in my own car. My real reason for the trip was the anticipated arrival of Beatrice's child in August. Also, I expected to go on another print pilgrimage with J. D. Metzgar and his daughter Mary Alice in September. So I wrote the following letter on April 6, as a feeler for a possible visit at Flat Rock while I was East.

Dear Carl, --

So your manuscript is in the hands of your publisher. I confess I was never so eager to see the finished book [Remembrance Rock] as this one. Perhaps because I have a feeling it was born in this old house.

The announcements here say that where M. G. M. enlisted you to write a book from which they might get a scenario you have in your volume given them enough material for twelve!

I hope to stop my car in front of your North Carolina home this summer when I come East. Mrs. Sandburg's descriptions a few months ago when she was here were very alluring, and no one in the world could have given me a more warm and genuine an invitation to do so. I think she could do it because she knows I know your ways, and that if you are busy on another tome I shall know very well that the only time I shall see you will be at the dinner table, and the rest of the time I shall amuse myself with the children and the goats. Anyway, I am sure that if I hadn't turned to music teaching I should have been a goat raiser! Remembering the blue rabbits you can believe that.

The enclosed is the sort of thing you get all the time, of course. Dutifully I send it on, though I told Robert [Robert Alden Sanborn, novelist and poet] the story that a number of years ago when I asked you how you had managed to turn the clock back ten years (since your previous visit when you had looked so tired and worn) you had answered with a grin, "By never answering my mail." And I believed you still kept it up.

My best to all the family and yourself,
Lilla

To this I received a reply on April 21 from Helga (at her father's instruction) inviting me to stay awhile whenever I came East. I replied to Helga with some details as to my plans. On August 2 Paula wrote, indicating that any time in September would fit in best with their plans, as Carl would be away the latter part of August and again in October, beginning with the first week.

Chapter XIII

So it was that I made my first visit to Flat Rock, North Carolina, where the Sandburgs were now living, in September 1948.

Before turning homeward from New York City I had stopped briefly in Greensboro to see my old friend Harry Lydenberg, retired director of the New York Public Library. He gave me carefully written directions for reaching the Sandburgs in Flat Rock. I have no doubt they were accurate and direct, but I saw a good deal more of North Carolina than I intended to before I reached Flat Rock late that afternoon. It was a fascinating country to travel through, however.

I phoned Mrs. Sandburg at Tryon and then proceeded on that road of a thousand curves to Flat Rock. I would like to take that beautiful drive again. This time, after my wild wanderings, I was too eager to reach my destination to appreciate it.

When I reached the country lane from which Carl's place, Connemara Farms, leads off I went by it for a mile or two. I passed many other beautiful estates, set far back from the road. After a little I realized from Mrs. Sandburg's directions that I had gone too far, and turned back. Nearing the main thoroughfare again I saw a boy of nine or ten coming along wheeling his bike up the slope.

"Do you know where the Carl Sandburgs live?" I asked.

No, he had no idea. I was sure I must be very close so I tried again. "Do you know where the goat farm is?"

He beamed. "Go right through those big gates, and you'll find it."

"Carl, your goats are more important to the country-side than you are! I shall get one of your booming laughs out of you with this story!" I said to myself.

Through the gates and around the double curve of the winding driveway, I caught a view of the house through the trees. The white mansion had once belonged to Jefferson Davis's Secretary of the Treasury, Christopher Memminger. It was built in the midst of two hundred and forty acres, Carl had told me, adding, "Ain't that a hell of a baronial estate for a proletarian poet!"

There had been a further change in Carl's plans, and he was not to be home during my visit. Mrs. Sandburg met me with a cordial welcome in the driveway. She had, doubt-less, seen my car winding up the hill. We went up the stone steps to the wide porticoed veranda, and through the right-hand door of the two front doorways. The door at the left, as I learned afterward, led into a large comfortable living room, with fireplace, davenport, easy chairs, and a grand piano. The door at the right led into what appeared to be a huge office. There were long tables and an enormous desk. They were piled with books and filing boxes. There was every evidence of a great deal of work being done here. But, as I learned later, this was where Carl kept his secre-taries busy, not where he worked himself.

We set my two small suitcases at the foot of the stairs, then went out-of-doors to meet the girls, Margaret, Janet, and Helga. Helga, the married daughter, had sepa-rated from her husband and was now living at Connemara with her two young children.

Mrs. Sandburg explained that it was feeding time for the goats and suggested that I might like to look around over the goat farm while she and the girls fed them. Helga was doing the milking. The breeding stock, Saanen, Toggenburg, and Nubian, was divided in separate corrals at some distance from the house. I watched and asked questions while they were fed. The herd of goats to be milked were in a central building, also the little kids, which had been separated from their mothers.

I did not know that it was the caretaker's day off on

Saturday, the first night of my visit. This was the one night in the week the family had all this work to do. It was the housemaid's day off, also. When we sat later in a beautiful modernized kitchen, and Mrs. Sandburg pulled delicious food out of the refrigerator, I was somewhat appalled at the generosity of her hospitality to me when she had so many things on her mind. The next morning the maid arrived from the village. Breakfast was served on an immense long table in the dining room, in such lavish quantity and such rich quality that I began to worry as to what a few days of this was going to do to my figure.

The room on the second floor at the front of the house was given to me. It looked off over the porticoed veranda, and the view was breathtaking. In the foreground was a large pool from which a fountain had been removed since the Sandburgs' day. Beyond it stretched a long slope of meadow grass, which in the Memmingers' time had doubtless been lawn. It reached far down to the distant road below. A little to the right was a little lake. Why should it suddenly remind me of the tiny "Noah's Ark" houses and wooden animals with which I used to construct miniature farm scenes as a child? A mirror surrounded by the all-too-green artificial grass would give the effect of this little lake.

"How perfectly placed!" I exclaimed.

"'Placed' is right," laughed Mrs. Sandburg. "It was part of the landscaping of Memminger's day, an artificial lake, made by damming up some of the springs which are found all over the place."

Later on I learned that it was stocked with fish. Some of the villagers came to ask permission to fish there. Beyond all this lay deeply wooded hills and the outline of mountains, among them Mt. Mitchell, the tallest peak in eastern America. As I stood in my room looking out upon all this I wished I could paint it to carry away with me and keep for always.

"Carl was to have this room," Mrs. Sandburg continued, "but he said this outlook was too much for him. He couldn't write here. So he has the two rooms on the right as we go toward the stairway. I'll show them to you."

They looked very much like Carl's top-of-the-house rooms on Lake Michigan, a workshop, with desk and bookcases, shelves and filing cases, all chaotic, yet with order in it of a sort. Apple boxes were ranged on top of each other against the wall to supplement the overflow from the bookshelves. Clippings were pinned about to the edge of shelves or to the wallpaper.

"Carl isn't really at home here yet. He hasn't quite found himself in these rooms. We have got to do something about it. We may put in a few more windows, move the wall back, and include some of the hall. I don't quite know yet."

The hall itself was an immense place. From my doorway to the head of the staircase on the opposite side I counted thirty-six steps. The big chimney in the center was no longer in use, the fireplaces connecting with it having been closed up. On all four sides of the chimney bookcases had been built. They were filled, too, from floor to ceiling. In all available space between doors, sometimes even out in the open spaces of the hall, stood huge filing cases or tiers of apple boxes, filled with books.

From my bedroom door, on the left going toward the stairway, were two large rooms belonging to Margaret and Janet. Margaret's was as filled with books as was her father's. She was, in fact, the librarian of the family. Many a time her mother and I, talking long over the dinner table, wanted to refer to some book. Margaret always knew where to put her hand on it. The girls had a small bathroom between their rooms. There was one off the hallway that I used.

Mrs. Sandburg's comfortable suite of rooms, consisting of a bedroom, living room and bath, was on the first floor. The bedroom was huge, with big bay windows. Twin beds were lost in one end of it. There were comfortable armchairs and reading lamps. I am sure she used it as her own living room as well, for the other room appeared to be accepted as a sort of workroom, with a sewing machine, and an ironing board left up all the time for convenience. On this first floor also, on the other side of the house from her mother's, was Helga's suite, a combination living room and bedroom, the children's (Paula and John's) room and nursery, and a large bathroom.

The dining room was immense, lined with books from floor to ceiling like all the other rooms. There was room to seat twenty at the big table. When there were few of us we gathered at Mrs. Sandburg's end. Off from the dining room, separated from it by French doors, was an office, lined with files and books from which all the goat correspondence and goat business was carried on. All here was in neat and easily understood order. This, if my count is right, made the ninth room on that first floor. I haven't mentioned a glassed-in conservatory off the front living room. Just now it didn't seem to be used for that purpose.

The meals at the long dining table were sumptuous feasts. Big beakers of goat's milk and cow's milk always on the table, pound slabs of both goat and cow butter, heaping platters of golden fried chicken, mounds of sweet corn from the garden, big pans of rich yellow corn bread, huge baked potatoes. These last were a meal in themselves when you spared no butter or the thick cream you spooned from the pitcher.

In the corner of the dining room the day I first arrived stood a bushel basket filled with apples of such flavor that they pulled you back for more. It was a house of abundance, where, I could easily see, an added guest or two could make no difference. Everywhere was comfort, the comfort of old armchairs from which no little hands or feet had to be warned away. There was the comfort, too, of every possible convenience and modernity in the kitchen. In the basement was a washing machine and an ironing machine, too. This basement had many rooms, rooms with storage for enough supplies to withstand a siege. Everywhere was the comfort of things much used and well worn. This did not link itself to elegance nor even beauty. Of this there was little, not even the care for arrangement and orderliness that, in itself, is a kind of beauty.

The entire household was an expression of Carl's idea of living. Paula, I feel sure, was not disturbed by it, and had even adopted it as her own. She laughed in unprotesting tolerance at Carl's accumulations. He didn't collect canes, he accumulated them, and his friends, knowing this, added to the lot. He could never bear to throw away a hat. Whether his friends gave him those also, I don't know. But there were five beautiful new ones in their boxes in the clothes closet of my guest room. After Paula's mentioning it, for fun one time I counted Carl's old hats and caps scattered throughout the house. There were seventeen when I gave up the count. Apple boxes, perhaps because of the possibility of their being converted at any time and anywhere into tables

85

or bookcases, were another of his collections. I laughingly asked Margaret one day what her father would say if we cleared out all the apple boxes in the upper hall and those scattered through his own two rooms. Her answer was, "I don't think he would like it," in a tone expressive of the fact that it had never been tried.

We had known, of course, that Carl would not be there during my visit. A few unchangeable dates on my Eastern trip, and a last-minute change necessitating his being in New York at the coming out of his new book, Remembrance Rock, had brought it about that he left Connemara Farms a day or two before I arrived. We talked over long distance that first evening. A few advance copies of his book had reached the family, and I read it late into the night that first evening.

It was arranged that Janet next morning should come to my room and waken me when she heard her mother stirring. But I was wide awake long before then. For a while I sat at the open window looking out at that view in face of which Carl found that he could not write. I was sure I understood why.

Then I got into bed again with Remembrance Rock. I think I was near the finish of the Prologue when Janet came into the room. "Why, Mrs. Perry, there are tears in your eyes!"

"Yes, there are. And if you tell your father he will understand that it is my comment so far on his book!"

All through my visit, when not involved in some activity with the family, I was absorbed in the book. There were wonderful passages, it had elements of greatness, but before I had finished I was deeply critical of it. It was Carl's first novel. Like Thomas Wolfe he needed editing. Catherine McCarthy of Harcourt Brace, his publisher, could have done it, but she was in Europe most of the time that it was taking shape. I had lunch with her in New York a few years after the book came out and to my surprise found that she would have tried to induce him to make some of the very changes that I would have wanted. She was in agreement that it should have been a trilogy: Revolutionary War, Civil War, World War. I am not sure, however, that she felt, as I did, that the book had not needed the framework in which the story is cast. The old judge is supposed to have written the story for his children. Carl could have done the story better without this framework.

I am not sure after this length of time that Catherine McCarthy agreed with me about the rock, for which the book was named, Remembrance Rock. It was the boulder under which were buried bits of the sand or earth from the various battlefields in our country's history. This was a touch of sentimentality that was not in the least like Carl, and that I, at least, found hard to take. At times there were magnificent pages, and for them one read on and on. I did, at least, though I later found many of my reader friends who didn't. My nearest lending library at home, a rental library, declared on account of the length of the book they could not stock it. Had it been in three volumes they would have had a long waiting list for it.

The reviews were good, for the most part. The literary world had somehow come to expect that anything that came from Carl Sandburg would be good. But today, as I write these lines many years later, if I were to ask any literary-minded librarian for a report on the book, he would say, "It was a best-selling novel that is not read today." I once asked one of the men at M. G. M. (whose children I was teaching music), one of the promoters of the book, why it was not made into a movie. "We wanted one film from it. Sandburg gave us material enough for twenty pictures. Frankly, we didn't know what to do with it."

My visit, as Paula said, would have been quite different had Carl been there, enjoyable though it was. I had been at their home on Lake Michigan enough to know how it would go. Carl would not alter his schedule by one iota. I should never expect to see him till dinner at two or two-thirty. We would sit long at the table and with a visitor there to call forth his best, all the family, secretary as well, would foregather and join in the fun. For Sandburg at his own table, as well as anyone else's, was good fun. If he had a guest who could give him a deep belly laugh he loved it. He treasured from his own experience the things that have made for laughter, and chortled as heartily as his listeners in the recounting of them. He was no monologist, however. He was a marvelous, inspiring listener. He drew forth the best from his guests, --at least that is what he always did from me. He made me remember things I had long forgotten. I was asked to his house because he enjoyed the play of minds we had together. Yet I was startled once at the compliment he paid me when he handed back to me my father's autobiography, the published part of it, which he had asked to see.

"That father of yours had the gift of the storyteller!

Having read this account of his I shall no more give you credit for yours than I would give credit to a leopard for having spots."

"You think me a good storyteller?" I asked in genuine surprise.

"You! You are packed with three-volume novels!"

That he had that illusion was the reason I had been a guest at his house so many times. It's been fine that he had it.

It is possible we might have sat over the table until four o'clock. I doubt if the housemaid would have intruded to clear the table. Now Carl would have risen and declared that he felt the need of a walk. He had always been a walker, and he now had two hundred and forty acres to roam over without leaving his own domain. I always suspected that he liked these walks alone, that he worked out many of his ideas at these times.

When he was living on Lake Michigan, getting very worn and tired and old, about the time he was finishing the Lincoln biography, he told me he had to give up the walks because they did not enable him to shake off his work. He had at that time turned to golf, he said, because he had to have something that would give him a complete change of thought.

There was one morning during my visit when Mrs. Sandburg suggested a walk, and I had an opportunity to see what entrancing territory Carl had to wander over. There were many springs, sometimes dammed to form little lakes, rustic bridges, sometimes just roughly made with logs, open pasture where the herds of goats grazed for as many as ten months out of the year. There were wooded glens. We didn't take the upper pathways, which would have given us a view over the whole valley. They are the most beautiful, Paula said, and suggested it for another day.

As we walked along we talked of many things. I asked about the people on the neighboring estates. Paula said they had been most friendly and Carl enjoyed them. In illustration of the inconsistency in our racial prejudices Paula spoke of the three little cottages belonging to three colored families, situated just across the road from the Robert E. Lee mansion nearby. It didn't bother Mrs. Lee the III in the slightest, though in the North it was not tolerated that the houses of blacks and whites exist in the same district. Yet at the Flat Rock railroad station there were separate waiting rooms, one of them marked plainly "For Colored People."

At a tea at Mrs. Robert E. Lee's not long before Paula told of a conversation that had amused her. There was insistence among some of these people who could not endure Franklin D. Roosevelt that he was not dead, that, like Hitler, he had been hidden away somewhere. It was the first time that I had heard this rumor, though later I heard it again in Washington.

"What reason do they give for such a spiriting away?" I asked in astonishment.

"Various reasons. One, that he had lost his mind, and that those close to him did not want the people to know it. Another, that things were too hot for him, and it was judged best that he disappear. They cite that after his death he was never seen by anyone, that his coffin was sealed. While this was being discussed at the tea another Southern lady burst forth, "There is absolutely nothing in it. I know the doctor who attended him, and if he hadn't died, that man would have seen to it that he did. I know the undertaker, too, and if there had been any life in him, he would have finished him!"

Later on I asked Margaret, then in her thirties, if she had attended this tea. "Oh, no, Mrs. Robert E. Lee isn't in the least interested in me. When she comes to see Mother and Dad she completely ignores me. She never even listened when I tried once to say something to her."

"And so you didn't try again?"

"No, I didn't," she smiled.

Margaret and I were much together during my visit. I was interested in her, and became very fond of her. She was a great reader; she was also an observer and a thinker. Much went on in that mind of hers that flicked to the surface in illuminating flashes. At the time of my visit she looked much older than her years. She told me with a resigned smile that just recently someone had thought she was Helga's mother. Helga was her youngest sister. It was not surprising. Her hair was quite grey. She used to slip into my room late at night. I was deep in the reading of Remembrance Rock and she could see a light under my door. I would put the book away and she would talk until one or two in the morning.

I learned that she had always persisted in her piano playing, and one day asked her to play for me. She played a Bach number from her music very nicely. I tested her out on reading something she had not looked at before. She did very well. She had gone far enough so that I could see that her piano ought always to be a wonderful resource to her. Yet next morning while I was seated out on the front porch deep in Remembrance Rock, I was appalled to hear her practicing in the next room. For more than an hour, by my watch, she worked on scales and arpeggios, nothing else. I walked into the room, and stood by the piano.

"Why do you work so long on these things, Margaret?"

"My teachers always told me I should, to improve my technique."

"Yes, if you were counting on being a concert pianist you would have to do a lot of that, and much more. But tell me, how often do you play for your family, or to other people who come here?"

"I never play for them at all!"

"Then let me tell you, Margaret, your scale and arpeggio practice in the past has given you enough technique for anything you will want to do, either in perfecting a composition you have memorized, or in sight-reading. You are like a person who is always preparing for living and never living. Give up the technique practice now and play. Pick out a few compositions you love deeply, and memorize them. Make them your very own, the expression of yourself. When you are quite sure of them call your father and mother in and ask them to listen to your short program. If you find yourself nervous and faltering it is because you are not quite sure enough. Your pieces need to 'set' and 'jell.' Don't be a bit discouraged, ask them to let you try again on them in a month's time. This will give you an objective, something definite to work for in your practice. Besides this, read over quantities of new music, improve your sight-reading. Good sight-readers always love to play.

90

"When I get back to New York I am going to send you a book that I have always found a big inspiration to my older piano pupils, Playing the Piano for Pleasure, by Charles Cook. You will love the first part of it, and when it gets too technical, stop. You said something the other day about starting music lessons again. At your age and with your past accomplishment you shouldn't be too dependent on a teacher. Work out a short program of memorized pieces first, and work to improve your sight-reading a great deal. All of that you can do by yourself. I have great faith in its being good for us to work by ourselves after we have reached the place that you have. It is time enough for you to go back to a teacher when you begin to feel a little dull and uninspired."

I questioned her about having memorized so little, and discovered, as I suspected, that she had no method. She got things, for the most part, by playing them over and over, developing a finger memory. I spent an hour or more with her showing her shortcuts, a memorizing based on harmonic forms and melodic patterns that begin in the head and work down to the fingers.

"Tomorrow let's memorize a piece together in this way. I can show you how much quicker it is, and how much surer you will be."

This conversation began a series of sessions at the piano that lasted to the end of my visit. When I saw the old-fashioned text books with which Margaret had been trying to teach piano to little Paula and John, Helga's young children, I was soon involved in showing her how to teach them as well. I gave them lessons, with Margaret observing.

With Janet, a childlike, sweet-natured girl, it was not possible to have the companionship that there was with Margaret. A tragic automobile accident of long ago had left its effect.

Helga, the youngest daughter, I hardly came to know at all. She was running the goat business, efficiently guiding the lives of her two small children, and working with her father's secretary, a young Jewish intellectual. She was for the moment completely absorbed in the distraction in her own life--her father's secretary, whom she afterward married. I am not sure that she even noticed that her mother had a guest.

91

With Paula there were many long talks, when her managerial tasks did not claim her. She was a keen-minded, sweet-natured woman. I have always felt that she was perfect for Carl. If she had a fault it might be that she was too uncritical of him. I am sure she did not feel that she had to entertain me. She knew there were a dozen things that I could turn to. Nothing presented itself in which I could have made myself useful, however.

At last came the morning I must leave. They all saw me off at the foot of the front steps, and Margaret rode into town with me to make sure I found the Automobile Club to get my directions for the drive to Washington. She left me in front of the Auto Club building. I had enjoyed her company; I hoped my visit had meant something to her.

Alice Thro, Carl Sandburg, and Lilla Perry in the kitchen, 720 South Kingsley Drive, Los Angeles

Chapter XIV

Carl's next visit to Los Angeles came the following year, in October of 1949. On October 17 there came in my mail an envelope with his familiar handwriting. It was written on an airliner, enroute to Seattle, telling me he expected to arrive in Los Angeles on Saturday and would stay over until the following Wednesday.

The days went by, and it was not until the following week that his voice came over the phone from the airport. I told him we had been expecting him and were ready for him. A friend he had made on the plane brought him to the house. It was eight in the evening.

I asked when he had last eaten. He had had a very substantial dinner around three, he said, and wanted nothing but a sandwich and some coffee. We talked until two. He had so much to tell me, so much he wanted to hear.

One of my first questions was about Kenneth Dodson, the man whose letters from the Pacific fighting front I had once shown to Carl. Had he ever got in touch with the man, I asked.

"Kenneth Dodson!" he exclaimed. "Why Kenneth Dodson was the reason for my going to Seattle! It wasn't for that program at the University of Washington. That was just worked in by my agent because I was going to be there. I owe Kenneth Dodson to you. And was he a gift! I was with him and his wife for five days. And he is more than a friend, now. He is part of my life!"

Dodson, he told me, was on a place near Seattle and

in spite of physical disabilities brought on by the war had gone on with his writing, producing the same powerful, poignant stuff we had found in those letters. While Sandburg was there, he had read everything Dodson had done on his book and was offering him every encouragement. They had had a long correspondence before the visit. It was evident from the deep feeling with which Carl spoke of him, that he was, indeed, part of his life. He inveighed against the attempts to "manage" Dodson's life by the local moguls of the Veteran's Administration. They were determined to "rehabilitate" him by the "book," but Dodson was intent upon writing Away All Boats.

While we were talking Tom Maloney, editor of Photography, called up from Chicago. He wanted Carl to attend the presentation of the Photography award to Edward Steichen on his way back home. He wanted him for a number of other things. Carl was evidently very fond of Maloney, and stayed in his penthouse whenever he was in New York. Carl was not in the mood for commitments however. I don't think he promised anything.

After the phone call Carl went back to that Seattle visit, where he had been with other dear friends part of the time. The woman, a writer friend from Chicago days, was slowly dying of some rare and little-understood disease. She was much on his mind, in pity and sorrow. On an impulse he put through a Seattle call, and talked with her and her husband, wanting to give comfort and courage. After his stay with them and with the Dodsons he had written Paula, saying that he had been near people who were clasping with feeble fingers the ramparts of life.

Sandburg was finishing a new book on Barrett, the Lincoln collector. In it he tells how Barrett used to sneak new acquisitions into the house by leaving them on a basement window ledge, retrieving them later by going down to his storeroom below stairs. He got a good laugh over my own tales of difficulty in sometimes getting my oriental treasures into the house. I told the story of the time I drove my car through the lattice of the tea garden because Everett appeared unexpectedly, and I had my car full of Japanese prints mounted on heavy cardboard. There was an exchange of many good stories that night.

I slept late next morning, till nine, but Carl did not appear until twelve. There was a leisurely breakfast. I think I knew pretty well what he liked. I had bought sweet butter, and dark bread, and had squeezed a beaker of orange juice with the pulp left in. It is strange how years after, one remembers those things. He spoke with deep feeling of little Mother, who, in the days when I would be away teaching at his breakfast hour, would bring out the things he liked. This was his first visit since she left us. We sat long over the coffee cups. Then while he went for a walk, I got in a brief half hour at the piano. I had a Debussy number half memorized. A week's neglect would have found it completely erased.

Then we drove to his sister Mary's. I had never met her before. Though she had lived in Los Angeles a number of years, I don't believe he ever made any attempt to stay at her house. Her son, Eric, and his wife, Charlene, and their two small children lived with her. He may have thought their household might not fit in very well with his hours of sleep. I insisted on staying in the car, reading during the afternoon, so that he might be alone with his sister. It had been agreed, however, that we would stay to dinner.

The evening was not altogether a successful one. Eric had asked in a number of friends to meet Carl, and it was a mistake. "What did they mean to me but a lot of names!" Carl exploded on the way home.

The next day's pattern was the same. This time, however, when I came down at nine I had my coffee, not waiting for Carl's breakfast at twelve. At two he took his walk, during which I rushed to the piano again to salvage my hard-earned Debussy.

At three Paul Jordan Smith and his wife came. I've known Paul Jordan for years. He's the author of a number of novels and was for years book editor for the Los Angeles Times. He is a better talker than he is a writer, I find. He and Carl had both attended Lombard College, and to hear them discuss with humor the many people they had both known there was good fun even though one did not know them. Both men had known Eugene Debs well and had good stories to tell about him. Paul Jordan, who is a born actor, actually looks like Debs whenever he quotes him, so Carl said of him later. Altogether it was a hilarious afternoon and we were sorry to have them depart at six. I had been listening to two perfectly matched raconteurs. Once more I was impressed with Carl as the evocative listener. He was as good a listener as he was a talker. And how far more rare a quality.

With my sister Alice's help we quickly had a good steak dinner after our guests left. I had fixed everything in readiness in the morning. (There was no cook at this time. The children had all left home, and the "paying guests" were gone.) Afterward I announced to Carl that Alice and I were leaving for a political meeting. He might catch up on his sleep or do anything else he wanted.

We were home soon after ten and the sound of laughter drew us to J.D.'s part of the house. J.D., as we always called him, was Judson D. Metzgar. He had been cataloging my own Japanese print collection, staying with us here at the house, when my husband had his fatal heart attack. He fitted well into our household, and the children had enjoyed having him around. My mother suggested he might be happier here in a real home than down at his hotel rooms. So it proved, and he had lived with us more than fifteen years.

It was up in J.D.'s suite of rooms that we now found Carl reading from Spectra, the book of verse that Witter Bynner and Arthur Davison Ficke had published anonymously years ago, tongue in cheek, as a travesty on the free-verse movement. Carl knew the book and had found it in J.D.'s library, a book out of print long ago and hard to come by nowadays. Our arrival did not stop the reading, though Carl went back and read some of the best things over again: "Upstairs there lies a Sodden Thing" and "Sounds." There were a lot of good ones, hilariously funny.

Alice had never heard Carl read verse before. His voice could be velvet. It had organ tones, and modulations, and two of these tones of pitch on a single word, such as no voice that I have ever heard. He might have been a great actor. He could often convey in just a look some character he was talking about.

After Spectra he tried out on us a number of his own unpublished things, for one, his whimsy of "The Yellow Paper Horse," which I did not like. It was as crazy as the most extreme modernistic painting, such as "Nude Descending the Staircase" or worse. When I told him so he said that was exactly what he had tried to do, a modernistic painting in words. But in addition, it had a mythology of his own, he said, which he thought he had just as much right to invent as the Greeks.

I loved the one he read, which I dubbed "The Collectors," about two squirrels who were obsessed with collecting nuts. Another one was about a fly, a flea, and a flick, discussing books and reading.

He had pages of such nonsense, which he read with great laughter. He called them, "Fables, Foibles and ___." There is a third word, which I cannot remember.

"Publish them? Oh no," he laughed. "These are just for myself to have fun with. As a matter of fact, someone did ask for them, to publish them, and I found myself drawing back with the strong feeling, 'Na, na, yer can't have these! These are personal. These are just for my own fun.'"

Before we left J.D.'s rooms that night Carl said we ought to send a note, signed by all of us, to Witter Bynner, telling him of the fun we had had in our session with Spectra. Next morning before Carl came down I ran off the following on my typewriter:

> Dear Witter Bynner,--
> Three wise men--one of them a woman--sat last night into the early morning hours listening to Spectra. It is true, of course, that Carl Sandburg's voice can make something out of anything. Yet after we had listened to most of them and hooted with laughter over many of them we decided that even if you and Arthur Ficke had written them with your tongues in your cheeks they were good stuff. To this we all subscribe.
>
> Sincerely,
> Lilla Perry
> Carl Sandburg
> J.D. Metzgar

I phoned the public library for Witter Bynner's address, and off the letter went to him. In a few days we got a good answer, "Emanuel sends greetings. How I wish Anne might!" (Arthur Ficke was dead.)

The next day after our twelve o'clock breakfast we drove over to Carl's sister's to bring her back here for the day. I suggested he take her up into his suite, where they could talk by themselves. In about ten minutes he came down again laughing. At sight of a comfortable couch Mary had thrown herself on it, and in a few minutes was fast asleep. "I come to Los Angeles partly to have long talks with my sister about our early life in Galesburg, and I look at her asleep!"

He sat down in the music room near my desk, and we went on from where we had left off. He had begun his autobiography and gave me a carbon of the first chapter. I felt certain that his seeing so much of his sister on this visit was to immerse himself in the atmosphere of his early days, which Mary shared. Through her he hoped to recover much that he had forgotten.

It got to be five o'clock, and Mary was still sleeping. Carl had said when he planned the day that he would take us out to dinner. Now he declared that anything I might pull out of the refrigerator would taste better than any restaurant food. It was Saturday. I had marketed for Sunday only. "We can eat up the dinner I had planned for tomorrow!" I laughed.

Carl followed me to the kitchen. My sister Alice came in and soon she and Carl were going fast and furious in a discussion of Ezra Pound. Carl admitted a weak spot in his heart for Pound and Pound's verse. "And as for his politics," he added, "it is just as if a younger brother had gone all wrong--but he is still an erring younger brother."

Alice challenged him to read aloud some of the Ezra Pound verse. He started in doing so, in a corner of the kitchen, insisting on my attention. My mind was diverted, meanwhile, by getting potatoes and a roast into the oven, and with my need of prodding him out of his corner to get vegetables and fruit out of the cooler behind his back! It was a hectic way to get dinner, and I would never have got it on if Alice hadn't helped me efficiently with all the table setting and other trimmings. We got him to admit finally that Ezra Pound cannot be read aloud. Even Carl could not compass that.

Mary came down at six-thirty, just as everything was ready to be taken from the oven. We had a jolly dinner, in which J. D. joined. When we finished it was time to take Mary home.

When we reached Eric's there was a Halloween party in full swing. Carl didn't want to leave the car, but compromised by agreeing to come over the next day if there would be no neighbors, no party, no people but the family. Carl growled on the way home about Eric (his nephew) and Charlene.

"They want me to give up my time when I come out here, and meet a lot of people who are nothing but names to me, yet they won't take the trouble to read any of my books. I sent them Remembrance Rock months ago, a year ago, and they haven't read a line of it yet! I'm not sure they have ever taken the trouble to read anything else of mine either. Don't they know that the best of me is in my books! I can't understand people who lay so much stress on having me around, and won't read a thing I've written!" He had exploded with much of this to Mary on the way over.

Now on the drive back we talked of other things, of people we had both known, of Alfred Kreymborg, whose last book, Man and Shadow, he said I should certainly get and read. He thought very highly of it. We spoke of Floyd Dell, whom he said was living near Washington, and writing absolutely nothing. I gave a little leap of joy to find that he had once known Charles Finger well. I, too, had come to know him well at an American Library Association convention, where he had been given the Newbery prize for the best children's book of the year, Tales from Silver Lands. We talked for a while of children's stories. I gathered that of all Carl's writings he has a particular fondness for his own tales for children, such as Rootabaga Stories or Potato Face. I had a feeling that it would have meant more to him to have received that Newbery prize himself than many another honor he has received. Yet my own children, avid readers as they were, did not care for his children's stories. I have questioned children's librarians and they have found the same indifference. Carl would have been deeply hurt had he known this.

The next day was Sunday. When we finished breakfast Carl said we had better go back to his sister's after he had had his walk. We didn't get started, however until after four, when he came in from his walk. Alice was with me, and they got into politics briefly. He teased her about her socialistic ideas, though he told me privately that he had once been pretty expressive of the same ideas himself. That he "had once been!" I had not discovered how much he had grown away from them, though my sister declared that he had lived too much with wealthy people in his later years.

We reached sister Mary's about five. Dinner was soon in order and this time we gathered in the breakfast nook. For hours we sat around the table listening to Carl and Mary tell about old times in Galesburg.

Carl was inclined to shrug his shoulders over the "birthplace."

"Paula says if the committee which purchased and restored it continues to be without funds for its maintenance it may possibly deteriorate into the condition it was in when the Sandburgs lived there. Now with new sidings and fresh paint she says it certainly doesn't look much like it."

"I hear," said Mary, "that it was your expostulations which saved the outhouse or privy when they were going to tear that down. You're right. It wouldn't have looked natural without that."

"I haven't seen the place since the restoration," Carl admitted. "I'd like to. But I'd want to do it at night--or in disguise. I thought they waited until people were dead before they did such things!"

I quoted something I had read in the paper that he had said when he first learned of the purchase of the birthplace, that he would far rather have people asking why in heck there wasn't a memorial to Carl Sandburg than have them go around asking why in heck there was!

Carl and Mary have little memory of this birthplace. The Sandburgs moved to another house soon after Carl was born. Mary said, to Carl's amusement, that they took her out of the cradle to put him in. There was vivid remembrance of the life that went on in the other two Galesburg houses, however. Chapters of Carl's autobiography were written from the talk that went on. When the Sandburgs moved to the last and largest house Mary was teaching school and had agreed to help with the purchase.

They talked about Carl's coming home from the Spanish-American War. When the men marched home from the station the whole town turned out to meet them. The men were a shabby-looking lot. Carl's clothes, like the rest, were worn out and grimy. Carl told about being given a room at home that first night in which there was a feather bed. He tossed and battled with it for quite a while. Then

100

he got out and finished the night on the good comfortable carpet.

The one who put ambition into the children was apparently the mother. His father, when asked why he did not learn to read, answered that he was always too busy. He didn't have time. The mother was a reader, and I remember years ago Carl's showing me a long poem she had written. After his program at the University of Washington a student's review in the college paper had said, "Carl Sandburg said his volumes of Lincoln were written about a man whose mother could not write her own name by a man whose father could not write his. Mr. Sandburg added: 'Is there substance in any thesis about the illiterate?'"

Then Carl and Mary did up the old characters in the Galesburg of their youth. It was another Spoon River Anthology, like the ones that years ago the Sandburgs had encouraged Edgar Lee Masters to write. Carl told of two old town bums. The schoolbooks of that day pictured what hard liquor did to your liver, and the other awful effects of alcohol. Carl, as a young man returning home after a number of years away, expected, of course, that these two old bums had both met their predicted untimely end. He remembers the jolt he got going through the park to find both of them sitting on a bench, laughing hilariously, still enjoying life hugely.

Was it any wonder that at this point Mary called for one of Carl's old folk songs, which he always sang with gusto. He had no guitar to accompany him this time.

I have led a good life, full of peace and quiet,
I shall have an old age, full of rum and riot;
I have been a good boy, wed to peace and study,
I shall have an old age, ribald, coarse and bloody.

I have never cut throats, even when I yearned to.
Never sang dirty songs that my fancy turned to.
I have been a nice boy and done what was expected.
I shall be an old bum, loved but unrespected.

In the midst of this the phone rang. It was Eric's English professor, wanting to know if he could come over and meet Carl Sandburg. In the face of Carl's gestures of negation, and his grimaces over the idea, poor Eric had a hard time. He knew he must put the man off, but he didn't want to hurt his feelings and he didn't want to lie. He made quite a mess of it, and there was even danger that the man might hear our laughter at Eric's difficulties before he got through.

"You ought to have turned that job over to Lilla Perry," Carl said to Eric when he returned to the table. "She's a practiced and master hand at it!"

"Gad, I'd better have been, or Carl wouldn't have continued to come to my house all these years!" I laughed. There had been plenty of times, I might have added, when, like Eric and Charlene, I would have liked to have won a little kudos by showing him off to my friends.

It was one o'clock when we started homeward, a half-hour's ride in the car. Carl was in high feather. He had had a good time. "You can see," he said when he came to leave, "how the intrusion of a strange person would have completely changed the mood, would have spoiled everything!"

Next day we drove downtown to change his reservations from one airline to another. When he signed at the desk the clerk asked, "Is it the Carl Sandburg?"

"Well, I suppose in a certain manner of speaking it is."

"Could we have some publicity on this, may I ask?"

"No," said Carl. "I'd rather not. And in view of those headlines yesterday with fifty-four people lost in an airliner, better not!"

As we walked away Carl said, "Considering that frightful airline disaster a few days ago there have been times in my life when I would have canceled this airline reservation. When I was in the midst of the Lincoln book I would have taken no chances. I would have had to make sure that I was around to finish that. Just now, well, it's an interlude between projects of work. If the plane went down it wouldn't matter as much as at some other times in my life."

On our drive home he told me about some of the writing projects he still had ahead.

He had a preface to write for a volume of his complete

poems, which Harcourt was to bring out. <u>In Reckless Ec-</u>
<u>stasy</u>, his first book of verse, <u>The Plaint of the Rose</u>, and
<u>Incidentals</u> were to be left out. There was to be nothing
preceding the <u>Chicago Poems</u>.

He had an article to do on Lincoln for the <u>Encyclo-</u>
<u>paedia Britannica</u>.

He was planning a one-volume Lincoln.

He had a mystery story in him, which he had titled
<u>Fallen Leaves</u>.

He had a new book of poems. He gave me a first
draft of one that he called "Nearer than any mother's heart
wishes."

He was speculating about a play to be called <u>The</u>
<u>Laughter of Lincoln</u>. Paula tried to discourage his attempt-
ing this, I remember. Play writing, we would both have
agreed, takes a long apprenticeship.

There was an outline in his mind of two short novels.

There was the book he wanted to call <u>Great Compan-</u>
<u>ions</u>. It was to contain chapters on a number of people whose
work and lives had interested him over the years. One of
these was the Japanese artist Hokusai, on whom he had asked
J.D. and myself to gather data.

There was, of course, always the autobiography.

"These things ought to keep me busy over the next ten
years," he laughed.

Once home again I suggested we go for dinner to a
quiet, good, little French restaurant that my sister and I
frequent.

"Ah, no. Let's stay home. Anything you would fix
would taste better than food in a restaurant. And if we went
there I couldn't burst out into song whenever I felt like it,
or give the rebel yell!"

While Alice and I were hastily pulling things out of
the refrigerator for an improvised meal Alice called for the
rebel yell. Actually, he said a bass or baritone voice cannot

give it. He substituted a Swedish call, which he and his
brother Mart used to greet each other with at long distance.
It was lusty.

He had found that there was a Marx Brothers double
feature that night, <u>Animal Crackers</u> and <u>Duck Soup,</u> and wanted us to go. It seemed he thoroughly enjoyed the Marx
Brothers, whom he knew and whose nonsense was just as
good in real life, he said, as anything they did in their movies. I never would have chosen to go to see them, but in
an enthusiast's company, appreciative of their kind of humor,
it might be different. It was! His laughter led the house.
I got more fun out of Carl than I did the show. The same
was true of my sister, I'm sure.

The next day included a dinner at the Clarence Dykstras', who were old friends of Carl's. They were old
friends of mine, too, though I had not seen them since Dykstra became Provost of the University of California at Los
Angeles. It was something for me to go back into University
House, so familiar to me in the days of Dorothea Moore's
life there. We left the Dykstras early. We had known in
advance that they had an evening engagement. Carl wanted
now to see some of the war pictures taken by combat cam-
eramen in the war. Many of these men had lost their lives
in getting these pictures. There were two parts, "The Building of the Burma Road," and the action in Europe beginning
with the Normandy beach attack.

We had seen announcements of the showing the night
before. I had said that I thought the pictures would be pretty hard to endure, with the realization that it was no Hollywood stuff but real action. Carl's answer silenced me. "I
guess if these boys could live through it, we could look at
it. "

They were powerful films. It seemed amazing that
war could be pictured for us just as things happened. The
next night, Carl's last, we went again, and took Alice with
us. Carl felt he must see them again.

Carl's airline change had made it impossible for me
to drive him to the airport. I had an engagement in Beverly
Hills. "Let me ride out for a way with you," Carl suggested.
"I'll get in my walk coming back."

As we drove along we talked about Paula. His sister,

104

Mary, and I had talked about Paula and the wonderful wife she was for Carl. She must often have wanted to change him, get him to pay more attention to his clothes and his haircuts, or to meet certain demands that he ruthlessly shrugged off. Perhaps she early recognized the necessity of his sometimes rather rugged self-preservation against the demands of answering letters and meeting people. At any rate, she seemed, with marvelous restraint, to have accepted him as he was, and let him alone.

We were talking of my visit to his family while he was away. "It was something to note that you have worn well with Paula," I put in at one point.

"I like your expression--'worn well.' She has had lots of occasion for anger at me," he laughed. "But our tempers haven't flown at the same time. When one of us was angry the other always seemed to be cool. I was blowing my top soon after our arrival at Flat Rock. I couldn't work in such conditions! I couldn't find anything I wanted. My papers were all mislaid. So I raged on. I'll never forget how coolly Paula said in the midst of my roaring, 'Well, perhaps it would be better if you went somewhere else!'" How he laughed as he told it! That had, indeed, set him back on his heels.

"Far enough now for my walk back," he said, and I drove the car to the curb. It was our "goodbye." Never before had he been so expressive of our good companionship. I felt the warmth of his affection for me, and his enjoyment in our many hours of exchanged thought. Would such days ever come again?, I wondered.

A few weeks later I wrote Carl the following chatty letter, on November 19:

> Dear Carl, --
> The books have arrived. Lincoln Collector came first, a really beautifully gotten out book. I spent three evenings on it. It is, of course, made up of the documentary material that you hope you are through with. But every little while some Sandburgian phrase breaks through. "Of the end of his young wife Nancy we know no more than of the vanished blue supper smoke that wreathes spiraling from a prairie log cabin."
> The Little Prince, since you said you had twice

read it aloud, I am saving for the same purpose
when we have a family get-together next Thursday.

Of course curiosity led me immediately to page
73 and 219 of the Lloyd Lewis book. Yes, he does
make you come alive in those word pictures [It
Takes All Kinds, Harcourt, Brace, 1947]. Perhaps
I have sketches as sharp among the transcripts of
life I may toss to the archives of the New York Library to be buried for fifty years!

Eric drove Mary over at eleven a week ago, and
we had a long day together. I kept her until nine
and then drove her home. I shall do that again.
Her task in caring for the children will wear on her
if she does not have a complete change once in a
while. Next time I will take her to a movie which
she seldom gets to. This first time we had to talk.

Please remember me fondly to Paula and the
girls. Get my young friend Margaret to hunt up
the chapter of my book which I called "What I
learned from my own children." Since you know
every one of them I really wanted you to see that.

It was fine getting the books. They are tapering
off your visit. You haven't quite left 720 yet.

Yours, as always,
Lilla

P.S. Of course one of the bits in the Barrett book
which I most thoroughly enjoyed was the way he
took, through the basement, of sneaking some of
his trophies into the house. I am sure that will
strike a hilarious note with many a born collector,
sure to be tied to someone who isn't!

Carl's reply of December 28 commented on the noteworthy days we had had during our visit--the pleasant short
trips and meals together, and the conversations--agreeable
and sharp. He would attest that I was one of the best con-
versationalists around, meaning my talk had variety and clar-
ity. He said that he could see the Hokusai book from his
desk; he held it dearly and would make good use of it. He
thought of it as a holiday remembrance from me and maybe
I would consider the Lincoln Collector in a similar way. He
said that he had read about half of my manuscript and hoped
to report on it soon.

By 1950 I had given up my piano teaching and considered that I had retired. So I turned to various projects I had long deferred, such as the reorganization, consolidation, and editing of my voluminous journals and letters, or the completion of my manuscript on piano pedagogy. Carl continued to write me occasionally and send his books along, and I would reply.

On April 27, 1950, he wrote, announcing the completion of the preface to his Complete Poems, commenting that strangely, or maybe not so strangely, Hokusai was featured at both the beginning and end of the preface. And maybe he wouldn't have been featured so strongly had it not been for that extremely likable book on Hokusai that I had given him, which he had read and re-read. He repeated that he had now read more than half of my ms. and would write about it. He mentioned that he would appreciate a copy of the Hemingway letter. [This letter--known to the Perry family and to a number of librarians--was Hemingway's reply to a letter from Everett Perry, inquiring why he used so many four-letter words in Death in the Afternoon.] He still recalled the four-day October visit pleasurably, and would assert that both of us had grown in Inner Grace, at least I had.

On Labor Day, I wrote him a lengthy and rambling letter that bespoke my relaxed frame of mind:

> Dear Carl, --
> I have just had J. D. run me about in his car (mine having been borrowed) to find some place that would be open this Labor Day where I could get the September number of the Atlantic. I had just heard of your article in it, and suspected it might include the lines quoting Hokusai which you sent me.
> I have just read it through very slowly. No one, I think, will be able to just glance through it. It gives one much to ponder, and the play of words alone will give delight to anyone who has ever made the attempt to string them together. I can imagine even the casual reader to whom you are only a big name sticking to the end of it, and saying as he lays it down, "That guy really does seem to have something on the beam!" In other words, I like it immensely.
> I'm at a new project just now. The book is out of my system--though it hasn't found a publisher yet. And I've kept at the piano till I have back my playing ease. I haven't tied anyone down to try it

out on him, but I could keep going for about two
hours now on compositions I have liked well enough
to have made my own.   Besides keeping these up
I am reading through all the piano literature I have
in my fairly sizable music library.   Awfully good
fun!   And just for fun, of course.
　　My new project is the typing out from quantities
of old quotation books which I have kept over the
years, the poems and sayings and paragraphs which
have stood the test of time for me.   To paraphrase
from your article which I have just read, much that
I found full of fine nourishment at one time I now
find of no interest to me.   These will be discarded
with the old note books they were in.   I began this
note taking when I was about fifteen, and still have
on the front of the first book this nice old jingle
which my father once presented me with.   This
wasn't the inspiration of my activity, but he knew
what I was up to.

> In reading authors when you find
> Bright passages which strike your mind
> And which perhaps you have reason
> To think on at another season,
> Be not contented with the sight
> But put them down in black and white
> For such respect is wisely shown
> As makes another's thoughts your own.

　　Later on my sister presented me with this ironic
bit from Marcus Aurelius Antoninus:

> "No longer delude thyself, for thou wilt never
> read thine own memoranda, nor the recorded
> deeds of old Romans and Greeks, and those pas-
> sages in books which thou hast been reserving
> for thine old age."

　　Against this last I have scrawled a vigorous "No!
This I have disproved."
　　When I get through with this enterprise I have
several others in prospect.   One part of me is having a wonderful time, freed from all responsibili-
ties, and doing just the things I love doing, another
part of me is miserably unhappy over this war.
This has grown to be a longer letter than I ought
ever to impose on you.   I wish you were here

sitting on the music room couch near my desk talking to me.

> My best to Paula and the girls,
> affectionately,
> Lilla

Back came a note from Carl, dated October 4, describing an enclosed clipping on Hokusai, possibly from the old
New York World, at some length.   He still felt guilty about
not having done a real reading of my ms., which he might
still be handing to the publishers.   He liked to hear how I was
spending my now independent time.   He might get to an L.A.
visit the coming year--he had no commitments to any particular writing jobs.

In a letter of December 19, 1950, I acknowledged the
receipt of the Complete Poems, and commented that I hadn't
gotten beyond the preface, which I liked immensely.   I had
gone over the index, looking for all the old favorites.

On January 31, 1951, I wrote again, thanking him for
the new Songbag, and commenting on how hard he was working.

In a letter written the following May 21 Carl spoke of
reworking a Segovia piece done in 1937 and in need of revision.   When finished, he planned to send me a copy.   He
said that he had been booked for a date in Houston the following February, and expected others on the West Coast.   So
he would see me then surely for a longer stay this time.   He
had completed his reading of my diary passages and thought
them remarkable.   Should I be visiting Mary, he would appreciate a report on my impressions.   Mary had had a bad
jolt, and her short notes had been a little weird.

To this note, I replied promptly on May 30, as follows:

> Dear Carl, --
> Spent part of an afternoon with Mary last week.
> After a visit which included Charlene and the chil-
> dren, she drew me off to her own room for a quiet
> talk.   She looks as though she had been through a
> pretty serious illness, and still has to articulate
> her words carefully, or they do not come as she
> wants them.   Of course there is no question of her

taking care of the children again. Charlene seems
very nice to her, and though I demurred about her
bringing in coffee and cakes, she whispered that it
would please Mary to have "a party" in her room.
So it was done. You said her brief letters came
a little weird. So does her speech at times. While
I was alone in the room with her she went to a
drawer and gathered up a package of clippings about
you that she has been hoarding over the years. "I
know you keep things that are written about Carl,"
she said, "and will you take these and put with
them. Everything about my life is so confused now.
It worries me to keep my things in any sort of order." I took them, of course, a little wonderingly.
You might like to look them over when you come
on. I am glad you have bookings for next February.

So my old doctor friend who periodically pro-
poses to me has beat me to it about getting a book
out. Do you remember my reading a letter of re-
fusal to him once when you were here? You were
so amused by it that you asked me to give you a
copy of it. He is a psychiatrist, and the title isn't
bad: <u>A Few Buttons Missing</u>.
Now it's time I ran.

Yours as always
Lilla

Carl was not too long in replying to this. On July 16
he wrote, asking if I would send on the clippings that Mary
had turned over to me. He thought that the obituary of his
father and other similar data might be among them. He
promised to send some of the manuscript he was working on
when it had been shaped up a little this fall. He had talked
to Mary and it had been thrilling to hear her voice coming
through clear and her speech better. He was sure that my
visit was of benefit to Mary. When he got to L. A. again
he hoped to stay longer and that we could have the longest
talks ever--which was not to say that we were not able to
maintain salutary Quaker silences.

Chapter XV

Carl's Houston date and others must have been pushed ahead, for the announcement had been in the papers for days that he was to give a program in Hollywood on November 11, 1951.

"We are going to have a visitor soon," my family told me. So it was no surprise to hear his voice from Houston, Texas, on Friday morning, the ninth, telling of his arrival by plane that evening.

My sister had offered to give him her suite during his stay and to come upstairs to the third floor with me. The fun she had at these times was worth it, she said.

We were both sitting in front of a brisk open fire that evening when Carl's taxi drew up. He set down a heavy Gladstone bag, a large briefcase and a surprisingly handsome overcoat, leaving them on a chair at the foot of the stairs. He didn't want to go up just then, he said, and joined us in front of the fireplace.

"When did you eat last?" I asked. "Alice and I can quickly throw on a dinner, or I have sandwiches and beer in the refrigerator all ready for you."

He said he had just eaten a hearty dinner on the plane. It was then eight-fifteen, and we sat there before the fire and talked until after one. Alice faded away about twelve. That night Carl's talk was at its best. Never with any of his best old pals could he have been any better. But he needed just the audience he wanted, else he could be as silent as he had been at his sister Mary's on his last visit, when she made the mistake of asking in her neighbors.

111

Early in the evening I, too, made the mistake of asking my friend, Mr. Gilbert Sterling, who lived with us then, as he was passing through the hall, to come over and be introduced to Carl. Carl rose and shook hands, to be sure, but he immediately returned to his talk with Alice and me. He ignored Sterling embarrassingly, excluding him so completely that the poor man had difficulty beating any sort of graceful retreat. I had seen Carl do that before, of course.

The next morning I safeguarded myself against a repetition of that occurrence. "Carl," I said, "there are some of my friends who live here in this house. They have seen your mail on the hall table. They know you are to be here during your stay in Los Angeles. They would be hurt if I did not introduce them. I can assure you, however, they won't absorb a moment of your time. They will pause just long enough for an introduction and that is all." "Of course. Of course," was his answer. And there was no repetition of his exclusion act.

The talk of that first night ranged far and wide. "I wanted this 'farewell tour' (it was the first time he has ever called it that), because I need at times to get away from the corner where I work. I arranged to have it hit Los Angeles and Seattle because I must see my sister Mary, again, and I needed good visits with you and Kenneth Dodson."

The name of a formerly well-known Western writer, Mary Austin, came up. I picked up from a table Agnes De Mille's Dance to the Piper, which had just come out, and read from it a descriptive bit about Mary Austin that had convulsed me.

> What did Mary Austin think? (about Agnes's dance performance at Santa Fe). She thought a lot of things about every fact that came to her attention.... She spoke like a sibyl ... "Never let the God be absent from your stage. Say your prayers before you dance." The Spanish tortoise shell comb in her bun gleamed in the moonlight like a horny crown. She had an arrogant, grey mustache, a droopy mouth, and a dictatorial manner. She did not converse--she issued bulls. She had broken the wilderness.

Carl chortled over this, as I knew he would. We had both known Mary Austin.

112

With all the work that he had always done, continuously over the years, it amazed me that he knew the work of other writers so well. And he said he was not a fast reader. "From now on I intend to read far less," he said. "My eyes, at seventy-three, are not as good as they used to be. They tire easily."

Perhaps his amazing knowledge of books and writers was because he remembered everything. The highlights of everything remained with him. It always astonished me that he remembered everything about this household, and seemingly everything that I had ever written or told him. For instance, he said, "I've been working in the New York Public Library recently. It's a really wonderful library, and I said to myself, 'Some day Lilla Perry's journal is going to repose in this place.'" I had forgotten I had told him that my journal, with a release date of forty years thence, was to reside sometime in its archives.

I asked him a question I had often intended to, whether he wrote his stuff longhand or directly on the typewriter. He answered as I thought he would, that it didn't make any difference. "A great deal of the time nowadays I like to write out-of-doors, and so do it longhand. Either way I have my own abbreviations that my typist has to understand." I've seen some of this writing with abbreviations and collected a few examples of it. To me it was quite unintelligible.

Next morning when Carl came down to breakfast I could perceive in the cruel morning light, as I hadn't the previous night, that he looked older than he did on his visit here two years before. The outlines of his face were not so firm. There was that perceptible softening of the flesh which comes with the years. Alice and I undoubtedly must have shown the same changes, though we were not as old as he was. Once before on a visit--just after the Lincoln War Years came out--he had looked haggard and worn, but the next time we saw him he had recovered from that weariness. My mother had exclaimed about the change in him. "Why, Mr. Sandburg, you look ten years younger than when you were here last. How have you managed it?"

Sandburg gave a laugh. "I'll tell you how, and perhaps it is no secret--by never answering my mail!"

To my question he said he had been in fine health and vigor, nothing the matter except the little trouble with his

eyes. He did for us some of the exercises he goes through
every morning. "They are relaxing exercises, not stimulating ones," he pointed out, and he had gone through them every morning for years.

During breakfast, to keep his eggs and bacon from
congealing, I took the conversation away from him. I brought
out the personal "anthology" on which I was working. I was
typing on good durable paper the lastingly interesting poems
and prose passages that I had culled from my reading from
earliest years. These existed at the time in scrappy old
notebooks. Some of the items were merely pasted in to save
typing. Many of the quotations were scrawled on loose sheets,
backs of envelopes, or anything else handy. In their exist-
ing form they would someday have been thrust into an incin-
erator. I was rescuing their values, and to me their values
were great.

We had been speaking of Henry James, and of his recent revival, and I turned to that clever characterization I
had once found in Imaginary Obligations, by Frank Moore Col-
by. Long after I had found it I read in Edith Wharton's autobiography that she also had discovered and delighted in it.
She showed it with glee to Henry James, but he was not
amused. There was also a delightful bit in Muriel Draper's
Music At Midnight, describing her first introduction to Henry
James and a telephone call. Carl begged for a copy of both
of them. Running through the pages, I found there were num-
berless bits that it was fun to share with him.

As an instance of unexplained genius I read aloud to
him the lines Gerro Nelson, my cousin's little girl, had written when she was fourteen years old, the morning after I had
taken her to hear the composer Henry Cowell give a piano
program. She had called it "To Henry Cowell" and she began it:

Last night I heard a strange musician.
He had frail fingers that did gigantic things.

It was a poem of some length, but in face of Carl's
concentrated attention I read every word of it.

"Let me take a look at that!" Carl exclaimed when I
had finished. I put it in his hands, and slowly he read it
aloud again. At the end he said, "With all the long apprenticeship I have served in writing verse, I doubt if I could

better that! I doubt if I could do as well! Listen to that ending. He read the last few lines again.

> He raised his fists
> And pounded them upon
> The gates of universes,
> And he didn't stop until
> There was a faint whisper behind the stars
> And the gates swung open.

"Tell me something about that girl. She wrote that at fourteen, you say! Have you anything else she wrote?"

"The story of Gerro would be a long one," I answered. "I was first aware of the genius of the child when she was seven. Her mother wanted me to listen to her improvisations on the piano. I heard them and went crazy about them. I was much more excited than her mother, who was a musician herself and a good improviser. But her mother's improvisations were merely charming Chaminade-like things, pleasing, but without the greatness of the music I was hearing from this child. The chords were new, stemming from nothing the child could have heard. Some of the melodies were heartbreaking, like nothing that could have come out of the experience of a happy child. Believe me, Carl, that music was to me more amazing than the verse that she later wrote.

"There came a time when her mother told me Gerro wasn't improvising music any more. She was writing poetry furiously. She was eleven then. When I saw her poetry I was impressed in only slightly less degree than with her music. It was mature, adult stuff, beyond possibility of her own experiencing. I'm certain that among my voluminous unsorted papers there must be some of her verse, and I'll try to find them while you are here, Carl. I do know that two of her poems were sent to Harper's Magazine by her mother and were accepted. I may have those."

"What about the girl herself?" Carl asked.

"That is quite a story!" I replied. I won't repeat it here, but after I had given Carl the few facts I knew of her wild career, he suggested that we collaborate on the most interesting tale he had heard in a long time, and call it "Lost Music."

Next morning at breakfast he asked to see the Henry

115

Cowell poem again, and read it aloud stirringly. "I wanted to see if it held up to the first impression," he said. "It does. I would be proud to have written it!"

My sister now came forward with the two published poems, "Routine," and "Country Girl," which came out in the April 1933 and December 1932 issues of Harper's. He read aloud "Routine":

No day can leave its mooring place
Without a tattered gown;
The cloth of tried monotony
Is slashed all up and down.

No wind, no tree, is fettered to
Tomorrow's little place.
A rose who wears a color twice
Is doomed to some disgrace.

The variable world is full
Of etchings finely done
A cabbage with a bustle on,
An apple in the sun.

"Damn that kid!" he exploded as he came to the finish. "If I could have discovered her before it was too late I would gladly have given the best there is in me to the development of her genius, as I am glad to give it to Kenneth Dodson. Carl then read "Country Girl":

I've just come in from winter cold
To go to bed, to twist and tuck
My knees all close below my breasts
Like some great comfortable duck!

And I shall eat a bun before
I go to bed, and I shall scrub.
The water will be warm and bright
Within the little wooden tub.

My lover waits below the wall.
I've been with him, and he shall wait
Until my face is at the pane,
No matter how extremely late.

And I shall comb my long black hair
And listen while my lover sings,
And think how desolate is heaven
Beside these sacred, human things!

116

"I don't suppose," Carl went on, "that there is anyone who has received over the years such tons of verse from aspiring poets as I have done, and I have never met anything as good as this!" He read "Routine" aloud again, probing each line for meanings, an action I stored up to throw back to him when next he tries any of his "cult of unintelligibility" stuff on me.

> A cabbage with a bustle on,
> An apple in the sun.

"Without the signature wouldn't any one suspect those lines of being Emily Dickinson's," he said, "and up among her best? I don't suppose she had ever read anything of Emily Dickinson's?"

"At eleven years old? No, I'm sure she never had nor her parents either. She didn't come from a literary family."

Then he read the lines she had called "Distances."

> All my friends on your long, rough voyages,
> My lost lovers and my children,
> My dead husband, and the adjustments of getting
> Back and forth to the cemetery
> On Sundays, --
> I laugh at your distances.
> Can I not think of Elizabeth in Rome
> Among the ruins,
> And see her red hair blowing in the wind?
> Can I not still feel the first kiss
> On my lips, reconciled?
> My children, though you may run half way
> Across the world,
> I have your fingers at my breast.
> I laugh as I sit by one grave
> And grieve my one grief.
> Maybe William is looking down
> And hating the fading flowers
> And the tears.

Carl read it as only he can read, to bring out the power and the beauty. When he laid it down he said slowly, "There is all the mystery of genius here." Then he lifted the page and read aloud again the lines:

117

My children, though you may run halfway
Across the world,
I have your fingers at my breast.

"Was ever motherhood better expressed, compressed
than in those few lines?   Naturally I like best the things she
has done in free verse.   I've never been able to express myself in rhymed verse, not effectively.   It always twisted and
thwarted my meaning to make the rhyme."

Alice and I promised to find more of the Gerro Nelson poetry before he left.

On the afternoon of his first day here I drove him to
his sister Mary's.   It was to be only a brief visit this time,
and again I insisted on staying in the car, letting him have
Mary to himself.   But it wouldn't work.   Eric and Charlene
came out and got me.   Carl was busy, off and on, with his
autobiography, still in the early period, which Mary, more
than anyone else in the world, helped him to reconstruct.
He had recently sent Mary the first big chunk of it.   Now he
got it away from her for me to read.

We were late in getting started home and had to struggle through all the traffic of the Saturday football game
streaming from the Coliseum.   Dinner at the house was a
late affair, though Alice turned to, and was a marvelous help.
Carl asked if we couldn't eat dinner in the kitchen.   When we
had finished, Alice and Mr. Metzgar, Carl and I, it was suggested that he might like to try out the guitar that he was to
use for his program the following night.   Alice and I had borrowed a good guitar from folksinger William Clauson, a member of the Swedish Society.

"Let's take more comfortable chairs in the living
room," I said.

"Oh, nar, the kind of tunes I want to try out fit much
better in the kitchen," was his retort.   So there we sat from
eight o'clock to nine-thirty listening to his folk songs.   I have
never heard him keep going so long on them.   Perhaps it was
because I called for a lot of old favorites he had not sung for
a long time.   He had lost the words for "Look Down, Look
Down Dat Lonesome Road."   But that I had in his own handwriting among my scraps, and found it for him.

Almost all the folk songs were new to my sister, and

I could sense her enjoyment of them. Back of it all for me was the remembrance of the rich, sonorous voice of Carl Sandburg in his forties. The amazing thing is that his voice at seventy-three was still so true. His guitar accompaniments would trouble a musician, and I have wondered often that he seems never to have taken the trouble to improve them. Perhaps he felt that an artistic perfection in his accompaniment background would render untrue the folk songs as sung by the people. They strummed their instruments as they felt like it. His audiences certainly have never seemed to mind.

The next day was Sunday, November 11, the day of his program. Before Carl came down to breakfast I had begun to realize that a number of his old friends might come to the house that evening after his program. I knew he had asked several of them whom he wanted much to see. Such a thing grows, and as I told Alice, when she found me making sandwiches in the kitchen, I didn't really know whether there would be five or thirty-five. I made sandwiches enough for the thirty-five and filled the refrigerator with quantities of bottles of beer, root beer, ginger ale, and Coca Cola. That was all out of the way before Carl came down.

The program that night at the Sartu Theater in Hollywood was one of the best I have ever heard Carl give. It was a heartwarming audience to begin with. When he came onto the platform, instead of mere applause there was an ovation, and the entire audience rose. The theater was too small; there had been several hundred turned away at the box office and so many phone calls for seats that later the management tried to get Sandburg to give another evening's program. But Carl wouldn't agree. Chairs had been placed on the stage, and for Alice and myself, who were Carl's guests, the only places that could be found were in the wings.

His program began by a brief talk on trends in modern poetry. I seem to remember a slight dig at the "cult of unintelligibility," which I had fun in using against him later. Then he spoke of the competitors of the book, and the disadvantages of radio and television in that you have to take what you can get. He pointed out the advantages of the book in that you can choose from hundreds on your walls, find the one to fit your mood, and for a final advantage you can skip portions of it.

He got his audience laughing when he told of the man who boasted of having heard two hundred Bob Hope programs, and when the program was due he went to it as to his dope. As he said the last words he made a jittery little motion with his hands, and it brought down the house. Discussing the program the next day he laughed over the putting in of that little gesture.

"If I say it without the gesture, the audience smiles; if I put in the gesture they laugh out loud. There are two strains in me, you know," he added, "one is the bum, and the other is the vaudevillian." We've always recognized the actor in him.

Then came the reading of some "pieces" (he called them) from his recent, as yet unpublished verse. The program ended with a group of folk songs. He was generous. His program lasted at least an hour and a half.

Fifteen showed up at the party at the house afterward. Carl knew he could ask as many as he felt inclined. It was a nice number. That evening it was Jake Zeitlin's young son, David, not Carl, who entertained us with folk songs sung to his guitar. Carl had done enough. It was the first time that I had ever seen him really wearied by his program. He sat close to the fireplace, as though he were cold. But his tongue was unwearied. He told many a good story, and every little while that great booming laugh of his would burst forth. It was two-thirty when the last guest departed, and we had eaten up all the sandwiches.

Next morning I, too, slept late, arriving downstairs only a short time before Carl appeared. Mildren Norton of the News came at two for an interview. Carl didn't like to give interviews, but he was very gracious to her for half an hour.

That evening we were picked up by Mr. Erwin Parnes, Carl's manager, who took us to the Philharmonic to see a Spanish ballet. Carl was in a mood to enjoy them uncritically; their gusto was enough to please him. But when we were sitting at a table in the Biltmore afterward I ventured to guess that the morning reviewers would pull them to pieces. Mr. Parnes nodded his agreement, adding that they were not a first-rate troupe.

While we sat there, laughing and talking, our waitress returned to our table. A lady, seated across the room, had asked her to inquire if he were not Carl Sandburg. The waitress directed her question to Carl, and he looked at her gravely for a second or two. "You can tell her that I am Robert Frost."

Eric called for Carl the next morning to take him over to Mary's. During this quiet stretch at home I went into the manuscript chapters of Carl's autobiography. I did not like the beginning. Carl agreed with me later that it should be changed. But when I got into the descriptions of his boyhood, the playing in the street, the characterization of his father, I read with enthusiasm, as did Alice, also. Here was the Carl Sandburg that the people loved.

The following day he was taken off for his program in Santa Barbara. It was lucky I had these times of respite during his visits. I found him so stimulating, so over-stimulating, that there wasn't an evening that we finished together that I could get to sleep without difficulty.

Friday night we drove out to Jake Zeitlin's bookshop in the red barn on La Cienega Blvd. There were two other guests, in whom Carl was not interested, and Carl, who always manages to do what he wants to, got Jake off by himself in a rear room after a while. He and Jake had years of reminiscences to dig up. Jake had put a bottle of very fine old liquor on the table, and I suspect the jollier things they dug up to laugh about the oftener Carl's hand reached out to pour himself a jigger. All the other guests departed but Alice and myself. Now, left alone in a front room with Mrs. Zeitlin, we heard Carl's voice coming from the rear room louder and louder, and his booming laugh sounding off oftener and oftener. It had been late when the evening started. It was now getting on toward one o'clock.

"What in the world are they having to drink in there?" I laughed. "I'm going in and pry Carl loose!" The minute I entered the room Carl knew what I was after. He reached out and clutched my arm. "Give me just five minutes more and this old alumni reunion will break up. I promise you. I promise you solemnly." As a matter of fact, he could have done nothing solemnly at the moment, but I beat a laughing retreat.

True to his word he and Jake joined us in five minutes, still laughing and joking. Jake was cold sober, but Carl had certainly had a few too many drinks. It was funny to me, for in the thirty-odd years I had known him, no

121

matter how tempting the circumstances, I had never known that to happen. Nor would it ever happen again, in all probability.

"Carl," I exclaimed, "Let's see you walk that crack in the floorboard. I don't believe you can do it!"

His feet could do it, but his voice and laughter were out of control. When we reached the car he scrambled in before me, and sat between Alice and me on the way home. His comments on domestic and world politics were perfectly coherent and logical and there was keen observation on everyone involved in them, but he was shouting them to Alice and me all the way home. People who came abreast of us at the stoplights looked at us. Before we reached our quiet, darkened house I said to Alice, "Stop the car on this corner and let Carl give out his rebel yell! After that, Carl, you must quiet to a whisper when we enter that sleeping house."

Alice stopped the car. Carl let out the blast of sound with which he and his brother Mart used to greet each other on the streets of Galesburg when they were boys, a Swedish call. After that he subsided to whispers as I had asked him. Next morning he remembered nothing about that last hour. "What did I yell about? What was I talking about on the way home?"

"Wouldn't you like to know?" I teased.

At different times throughout his visit, he had delved into his briefcase and brought out some of his later, unpublished "pieces." Sometimes he handed them over to me to keep. He did not seem to realize how completely he had entered into the realm of "unintelligibility" in some of them.

When he had finished reading a new poem to me one day I said, "Carl, of course, you are going to hate me for asking this, but what in heaven's name does that poem mean, what are you trying to convey?"

He showed not a bit of impatience with me. He looked thoughtfully off into space for a moment. Then lucidly, in phrases of real beauty, he paraphrased slowly what he had just read.

"But, Carl," I exclaimed, "that is beautiful and I see what you are trying to express. It means something to me!

122

Must it all be so hidden in the verse?" He looked at me questioningly, and did not answer.

There was one particular "piece," "The Triumph of the Yellow Paper Horse," which seemed packed with meaning for him. I had heard it on each recent visit in different versions. He rolled it lusciously on his tongue. I think it grew more and more unintelligible. Carl defended it as though it were the favorite of all his recent output. He read it aloud with zest more than once on this visit, and it did not grow on me. I reminded him with what care he probed for meanings in each line of Gerro Nelson's verse. "Don't think for a moment that that is not what your readers do to yours. I know you like this yourself. Can't you give me some clue as to what you want to convey in it?"

He treated my request with seriousness. "I think I had five intentions in the writing of that," he said.

"Hold on a minute," I interrupted. "You have given me those five intentions before, and I need to mull over them. Do you mind if I write them down?" He didn't, and I scribbled on a pad as he outlined them.

"One, to experiment with myth making. The Greeks made their myths, so did the Norsemen, so do all peoples. Why shouldn't I?"

"But no one person, Carl, can create a myth. It takes a whole people."

"But someone must begin it," he laughed.

"Second, to create actions and pictures that would interest children." Then he added, "I've tried 'The Yellow Paper Horse' on the children at home, and John and little Paula laughed at it and enjoyed it. I looked over at Paula, and she was nodding her head and smiling."

"That doesn't mean a thing! Paula was nodding and smiling because you were giving the children fun. With your dramatizations and the inflections of your voice you could take the multiplication table and make children love it. But the first time you see any child from five to fifteen sitting down alone and enjoying 'The Yellow Paper Horse' let me know about it."

"Third, to form with words and images something that

123

would parallel the feeling of an abstract painter in line and color. I rewrote this piece the last time just after I had visited an exhibition of abstract design at the Museum of Modern Art."

"In this intention, Carl, I do believe that you succeed."

"Fourth, to convey some moments in the story that would have the spirit of the awful transiency of the Universe. The shelf of the Niagara Falls is slowly wearing back, so many inches a year they tell us ... There will come a day when the Rocky Mountains are no more."

"I admit, Carl, this is vaguely suggested, but hidden among so much confusion that one would have to be told what to look for. Who wants footnotes to a poem?"

"Fifth, this is nothing calculated, but I am indulging myself, and I hope the reader will be indulging himself in a blue bath of maroon phantasies, 'spikes of brass married to spokes of gold, ribbons of sleep crossed with battle cries.'"

To this last I could not reply. I think perhaps he does this for the very few.

Pondering these things and the trend of quite a bit of his later free-verse writing I sat down at my typewriter the next morning before he came downstairs to breakfast and wrote off the following:

From the Biography of Carl Sandburg
by A E Futurs Published 1990

In his later work he departed from the direct appeal of his earlier verse. This poet, whose first volume had been carried around under the arms of students, and whose message to the people (yes) had made him the best-loved poet in America, now joined the current "cult of unintelligibility" and he cared not a hoot that his meanings were known only to himself and God.
There were those among his many devotees who tried vainly to form Sandburg Societies in the spirit of the Browning Societies of the early part of the century where every careless phrase was submitted to micro-scopic scrutiny. But the impulse toward greater and greater speed in automobiles and jet propulsion had had its effect upon the human mind. Whatever poem

it failed to solve upon a third reading it cast aside. It is regrettable to the mind of this critic that the later poems of Sandburg are now read only by the writers of abstruse literary theses.

For there is value in the effort of those who in words have groped with the antennae of the spirit into realms through which the human mind has never traveled. Through such only are advances made. But they must build their lines of communication strong, else they take their flight alone and none attempt to follow.

Carl laughed at this when he read it. But he folded the carbon copy and it went off in his portfolio.

One morning, pawing around among papers for things to read to Carl at breakfast, I came across a sheaf of scribbled notes that I had written to Norman and laid on his desk in the unheated garage room he had insisted on having when he was a Cal. Tech. student. It was probably so he could come and go as he wanted without supervision from me as to how he looked. It was always terrible, I remember. I had rescued these notes from his desk drawer long after he left home. To my knowledge he never threw anything away. I had recovered my sense of humor about him by this time, enough to find them funny.

"Norman, if you will empty your pockets and hang trousers over a chair at night instead of dropping them in a heap on the floor, I'll pay for the pressing. Otherwise, I am going to take it out of your allowance. Stockings off floor, please, not dropped just anywhere!"

"Norman, you have an alarm clock and you've got brains enough to use it. I can't ask Beatrice to run out to that garage room to wake you mornings."

There were many more. Those days were far enough away so that I, too, could get a good laugh out of them. Carl had always recognized Norman's faults as pretty much what his own must have been in his youth, complete obliviousness to personal appearance and to comforts. At any rate he always had a particularly warm spot in his heart for my youngest son. He took from his pocket a copy of "The Triumph of the Yellow Paper Horse," wrote a note to Norman on it, and said, "Send this to him!" He had previously asked for copies of Norman's incomprehensible articles on psychometrics in The Journal of Psychology, and when he asked me to send on this note I said, "Norman will probably think you are exchanging his work--incomprehensible to you, for some of yours, incomprehensible to him." I knew that Norman was as little likely to make any reply at all as Carl himself would be.

One of the good times we had was over my collection of Japanese netsuke. Some of them are masterpieces of sculpture in miniature. I often told Carl that, like the first character in Remembrance Rock, he must have been a wood-carver in some previous incarnation. Around this house he was always more aware of fine wood carving than of any other art treasure I possess. This time I had a lot of new acquisitions in the netsuke collection that he had not seen. Of course, I do tend to get finer and finer ones, and his enthusiasm was delightful to share. He reminded me that years ago I had given him a carved wooden dog, which he said he always kept on his desk at home. I remembered it. It was the first netsuke I had ever owned and it had traveled around in my pocket for many days. I must have liked him pretty well to have given him that dog!

"Let's have another session with these," he said, as I put the collection away. "I want to go over them again when we have more time, and look at them more slowly." It was one of many things we intended to go back to, and didn't.

Erwin Parnes, his manager, had asked to drive him to the airport, and had invited me along. On the way Carl enumerated the things I had promised to send him out of my personal anthology. "Don't forget those amusing Henry James items," he reminded me. "And I want to see everything you can find of the Gerro Nelson material. I want to see every scrap. We must do something with that. We'll collaborate in some way on it. Will you promise?"

"I'll find everything I have kept and toss it in your lap." Then I added, "In time, Carl, you will get all those things you have asked for. But you must know that writing to you, or sending anything to you is like tossing a ball which one never receives back. Why don't you develop a postcard habit, and write, 'Got it. No good. C.S.' That would be better than blank silence."

126

"You say this to me!" he exclaimed, "And I write more letters to you than to any other woman in the United States!"

A wonderful visit had come to an end. I had enjoyed every minute of it. But I felt like a yellow paper horse. I went home, tumbled into bed, and slept for twelve hours.

Chapter XVI

Copies of quotations Carl had liked and asked for from my anthology were very shortly on their way to him. The Gerro Nelson material was a different matter. Gerro's father and mother were dead; it was years since we had had any news of the girl herself. I had vivid remembrance of the sheaf of poems her mother had salvaged. If I only knew where they were today! From a batch of newspaper clippings and pictures I could piece together much of her life in Hollywood.

It was distressing that my sister and I could find only four poems out of the continuous flow that I knew had come from her pencil during her teens. I remembered the theme and the wonder of so many of them. I am sure I would always have had some remembrance of that poem on Henry Cowell if I had seen it only once. Yet exact lines like these would have been lost:

Have you ever seen a cloud race across the blue,
And gather the sun in its shawl, as it went.

Carl wanted a story of her life. No fictionalized character could ever have led a wilder, more adventurous one. We are warned, however, that you cannot take facts and turn them into fiction with a transmutation of the material. And her story had no ending. I did not know whether she was still alive, or what her fate had been. Certainly no fiction could have been more tumultuous than her own life, but my knowledge of it left off in midair. I could not even contrive an imagined ending. Why not leave it there--in midair? But to leave the ending open and unsolved, I needed some sort of "frame" for the story--perhaps a dead woman, and wonderment on the part of the teller of the tale as to whether she were not the girl who had disappeared. The narrator's speculations would bring to the fore all the facts of the girl's life, and these I planned not to change an iota. Carl would, at least, have in his hands all the material I did.

I did the best I could with "Lost Music." When I sent it to Carl I wondered what he would do with it.

In a note written on December 7 Carl commented on the fine and noteworthy sessions we had had. He felt that he had come to know Alice and me in extended ranges. He commented on his week-long visit with Kenneth Dodson, during which he read all but the two unfinished chapters of his book. His personality was evident in the overtones of his writing, and Carl was going to back him to the limit. He asked that the experimental piece he enclosed be kept confidential. He compared Gerro to Sappho in the irregular pattern of their lives, and he found the examples of Gerro's work as good as the best of Sappho's. He concluded with the story of a Chicago doctor, with whom he spent a convivial all-night session at the doctor's office. The doctor friend took him for the three-hour drive out to the old Sandburg home at Harbert. Arriving at sunrise, with the eastern sky all the colors of the rainbow, the doctor said smilingly, "There is something forgiving about the dawn." In a postscript to the letter, Carl mentioned an enclosed memo on "Confusions," which he characterized as having neither "Paper Horse" nor "Spun Glass" in it, being entirely comprehensible.

Carl wrote another note, undated, which must have arrived soon after that of December 7, and may even have been received after mine of the 16th of December had been sent. He approved of the Gerro story and suggested doing the "Masked Pianist" the same way. Add to these the as-yet-unwritten Percy Grainger story and "If my wife dies will you marry me?" and Carl promised to show them to Harcourt and report if they see a book in them. These were stories I had told Carl about during his visit. They also were factual tales, but I felt no impulse to work on them.

On December 16 I wrote Carl the following:

Dear Carl, --
Along came "Spun Glass" and "Confusions" yesterday. Realizing how much one hopes for quick reactions to pieces recently spun, I telegraph you immediately that I like them--BOTH.

129

To like "Spun Glass" may seem an inconsistency.
But for me there are two kinds of unintelligibles:

At some of them you gaze into their dark, and
there comes a sort of adjusting dilation of the mental vision. Astonishingly you see, though what you
see may forever remain untranslatable.

At others, you peer and peer, and squint and
squint--and nothing happens. "Spun Glass" is not
of these.

Many thanks for sharing. I am so glad to learn
that Dodson holds up to your first feeling about him.

Yours,
Lilla Perry

A week later, on the 23rd, I wrote again.

Dear Carl, --

You'll be with us at our Christmas party, not
quite as you told Carl [John Carl, Helga's boy] and
little Paula that they would be in two places at once,
but the record program came today, and Norman is
going to bring in on Christmas a recording machine
that will take those slow records. So after the dinner, and the distribution of the gifts, on comes your
program for us. It will be a delightful surprise for
everybody.

Norman and Frances (who are staying at her
mother's) spent last evening with us. Such fun and
laughter we haven't had since you were here. You
should hear some of Norman's new shaggy dog stories! They were much disappointed at the loss in
the mail of your note to them. The second note
which you wrote to replace that lost one came in
the mail today, and I can assure you they will be
glad to get it. Norman took away "The Yellow Paper Horse" with him to mull over it.

I'm glad if you liked the Gerro story. "The
Masked Pianist" appears to be factual, and I am
afraid too generally known. "If my wife dies, will
you marry me?" was turned on mainly to keep you
busy at your breakfast table before it got stone cold.
The Gerro story I had great interest and pleasure
in trying to put together. Haven't you any shots of
criticism on it? I kept only the carbon. What
would you think of shooting it on to Harper's in
which the poems were originally published?

Gratefully,
Lilla

Even if I could do anything with the other two
stories which you mention, the three at perhaps
8,000 words or less would run to only 24,000, not
a salable length I think.   I might have to cut the
present 8,000 words of the Gerro story for Harper's
Magazine, but if they liked it at all they would give
me a chance to cut it.

On February 19, 1952, Carl wrote me again, commenting, to begin with, that I should understand why he lived in
an uproar that never settled down, and incomplete work that
stayed incomplete.   He enjoined me to read Van Wyck Brooks's
The Confident Years, and especially the last two chapters,
which he felt had a special message for me.   He acknowledged receiving the ms. on the Lost Girl, and was considering it.   He felt sad that so little of her amazing writings had
been preserved, but glad of the few fragments that remain.
He hoped to send me a newsy letter soon.

To this I must have replied soon after, but the letter
was not saved.   In it I must have told about a possible lead
to Gerro, for in an undated reply, Carl said that Alice and I
were sharp, and he offered a bet that we would locate her
yet.   He felt that the odds were heavy that it was Gerro in Today's Woman.   And we had written instantly, which was the
next logical move.

I replied sometime in March, commenting on the horrible picture of Carl accompanying the Dallas Morning News
article he had just sent me.   Not a word as yet, I reported,
from Today's Woman's Gerro Nelson, and I had certainly
baited her in my note.

On June 26, 1952, I wrote Carl the following note on
a postcard:

Dear Carl, --
Our good old friend Hokusai [J. D. Metzgar] went
back to Chicago ten days ago to be with his daughter and go into a hospital for the removal of a
growth in the intestines.   He has come through the
operation all right, but I have not yet found out from
his daughter the important thing--whether it was
malignant or not.   He is going through a painful

131

convalescence, opiates not working very well, I
understand. One of your "veni, vidi, vici" kind of
messages on the enclosed postcard would give him
a boost, I am sure.

Yours as always,
Lilla

Are you helping to redeem television yet?

Carl obliged with a pleasant note on July 10, offering
J. D. the profoundest best wishes and hoping for his restora-
tion to good health. He hoped that for a long time yet that
J. D. would live on as a much-loved elder.

On October 9 I wrote another discursive letter to Carl.

Dear Carl, --
Thanks for the postal to J. D. He was pleased,
I know. He is home again now, and almost like
his old self again.
Rhys Williams, who keeps me supplied with your
press notices, sent me the enclosed the other day.
Why the St. Simeon Stylites I don't know. But his
comment was, "Nice opposites. The saint achieves
fame by doing nothing. Sandburg by doing everything. "
You can imagine the reluctance with which I gave
Paul Jordan Smith your address a while ago, knowing that his purpose was to inveigle you into a sort
of Peterborough project down near Malibu, when you
come out here in January. Parnes promises you
for January, and I hope this time his experience has
taught him to get a larger place.
I had a letter this week from the New York City
librarian asking for my lifelong manuscript journal,
to be kept among their manuscript files and released
at whatever date I may set. I don't know him, but
his predecessor, who is a friend of mine, must have
told him about it. As a matter of fact I have been
working on it all summer. As a story I have been
able to supplement it from the packages of my letters that I found among Mother's possessions in the
attic. It looks as though she had never destroyed
any of them. The project goes slowly. I have only
just finished the college years, and began today on
this visit to Dr. Mary Walker on her farm, where

132

I took dictation by the hour on material for her memoirs, her imprisonment during the Civil War, her encounters with Walt Whitman and many interesting things. I kept my own carbon of the stuff, and to my knowledge none of her material was ever published. Are you old-timer enough for her name to mean anything to you? She had personal letters from Lincoln which I saw.

At the present time--though I may discard the idea--I am occasionally putting in comments on events or feelings of long ago from the vantage of the present. They might be entered in rubric! A few days ago I was transcribing a period of intense grief. I can remember it to this day as almost the worst I ever lived through. And I made this comment from today:

"Oh, that mad grief of Youth! There is nothing in later years that so lacerates and sears. It is fortunate that nerves, heart and flesh have the strength and the elasticity then to bear it. For grief is taken on the raw, uninsulated soul, with none of the philosophy of acceptance which develops as a buffer in our later years against disillusionment, disaster and death."

But I am already one page too many. I wonder what you are working on at the present.

My love to all your family.

Sincerely,
Lilla

Carl's next letter to me, written on October 14, was probably mailed before he received mine. The reasons for its being written were immediately evident. He started off: The book [Always the Young Strangers] was finished, and totaled 166,000 words. Harcourt had informed him they would publish it on his seventy-fifth birthday--January 6. The advance copies for the book reviewers had been mimeographed and were about the size of a New York phone book. One of these had been sent to Mary, where I could obtain it if I wanted an early opportunity to read it. Carl had planned to speak for Adlai Stevenson twice in the last week of his campaign, and believed that he would make a great President. He confirmed the fact that he had a speaking date in Los Angeles the next January. Carl was still exclamatory about my journal, which he felt would be worked upon and be famous beyond the best-sellers of our times. Helga, her husband,

and the two children had moved to Fall Church, Virginia, where he was teaching English at the high school level. Consequently there was plenty of room at Connemara, and better food than ever, so I was welcome for a month or two of vacation any time. He had thought of several letters to write me, and finally one of them was written down. He sent his love to me and the house and the kitchen of fond memories.

My reply to this peppy communication, though undated, must have been written on October 18 or 19.

Dear Carl, --
I was so pleased to get your note yesterday that I am inflicting a reply, even though I suspect your next communication will be a wire of arrival in January--unless that damn Malibu colony gets you.

Of course, I'm for Adlai, too, but I took great pleasure in showing your note to J. D.

Think of it, I am now spending as many hours at my typewriter as you are, and that is saying something. I have just finished an account written up in much detail of a ten days' visit to the farm of Dr. Mary Walker, whom I met on a train when I was just out of college, and who wanted me to help her with her memoirs. She had letters from Abraham Lincoln and there was the testimony of an old soldier who worked for her that gave evidence of the courageous work she had done as a surgeon in the Civil War before she became the rather ridiculous, notorious figure later, known only because she wore men's clothes. The account is a character study, really. Of course I have all the material she dictated to me, part of it her experiences as a prisoner of war for three months, which I am sure never saw print.

Just now I am working through the year when I was teaching night school in New York and attending a School of Journalism held in the World building. It was a humorous, gay adventure, or at least so it appears in the reporting of it. It all sets me back almost fifty years, and I am having enough fun doing it to make it worth while even if some misadventure burned the whole thing up after I get through with it. There are not many people, are there, who can live through a lifetime twice? Well, maybe I'll get to some parts I won't want to.

I'll give "Sandy" three weeks on the book, then

134

I'll go over and try to get it away from her. I
don't even know what you've been up to this time,
novel, play, or "Great Companions."

Yours, as always,
Lilla

But Carl Sandburg never made it out to Los Angeles
for his January speaking date, as his time was preempted for
the January 6 celebration of his seventy-fifth birthday in Chicago. I have a box full of clippings that my family and friends
sent me from many cities where that even made newspaper
headlines. Governor Adlai Stevenson had proclaimed a Carl
Sandburg week in Illinois, which culminated in a birthday party dinner in the Crystal Ballroom of the Blackstone Hotel in
Chicago at which five hundred people attended. Similar dinners in other cities were held honoring him, one even in
Stockholm.

The day before the event I was called up by Carl's old
friend Jake Zeitlin, the bookman. There was to be a gathering of Carl's old friends and admirers at the Red Barn on
La Cienega, Zeitlin's bookstore, to celebrate the birthday.
There were to be a number of speakers, and, as Carl's nearest and oldest friend out here on the Coast, I too was asked
to be one of them. With all the wealth of material back of
me from which to draw tales and pictures of Carl, I readily
accepted. I had no written speech, of course, but I talked
for half an hour from a few topic headings I had on a card.
I do remember the incident I closed with:

Five or six years ago Carl took me to Ingrid
Bergman's to dinner. He and Ingrid, both with
Swedish backgrounds, had known each other for a
long time. When invited, Carl had asked if he
might bring his hostess. This was long before the
breakup of the Lindstrom family, for little Pia, the
daughter, was only five. There were just the Lind-
stroms, Carl and myself. We lingered long in talk
over the dinner table, and every little while, Carl,
fearing that grown-up talk might be getting tiresome
to little Pia, would turn his entire attention upon
her, and delight her with some of his tricks. Carl
has a way with children; I had many times seen him
work his fascination on mine. When we finally rose
from the table, it was late enough for us to take
our leave. Pia sensed that her new friend was

135

about to depart. She threw herself pleading into her father's arms, and exclaimed breathlessly, "Oh, can't we keep him, Daddy? Can't we keep him?" Here, tonight, to celebrate Carl's seventy-fifth birthday, little Pia's sentiments are shared by all of us. We want to keep him. When he was last in Los Angeles he told me of the number of writing projects he has yet before him. "Enough to keep me busy for the next ten years," he laughed. We all want to keep him for as many more years as we can.

Later in January I received a copy of Always the Young Strangers from Harcourt, and dashed off the following note on February 1:

Dear Carl, --
Thanks so much for the book! It has been next best to having those long breakfast conversations that I had so much been looking forward to. For the book has been much like yourself talking.

All my friends, east and west, have been sending me reviews of it. I must have a file now as big as your own. Every one, with only one exception, has been most laudatory. Caswell, who is now head of the Burbank library near Los Angeles, tells me that already there is a long waiting list in his library for the book. Parnes tells me that the seats for that big auditorium were going fast.

I am myself putting in six or seven hours every day at the organization and retyping of that voluminous journal material. Did I tell you that the New York Public Library director, whom I don't know, wrote me asking for it, and agreeing to put a release date on it? I think Dr. Lydenberg put him up to asking for it. There would have been chunks of it to read to you at the breakfasts. I've found surprising and amusing things long forgotten.

I'm going out to see Mary soon to get her reaction to the book. I'll bet she loved it.

Lilla

With the remarkable memory you've been exhibiting do you remember the years and the number of times you've been to the Coast? 1921, the first time.

136

Another note, on the 17th of February, was occasioned
by one of Carl's TV appearances.

Dear Carl--
That was a wonderful half hour with you last night
from 10:30 to eleven out here. Alice and I hovered
over her television set, not wishing to miss a word.
I don't think we did. I noticed, of course, when
you were asked for a poem that you especially liked
that you didn't give 'em "The Yellow Paper Horse!"
There was only one thing about the broadcast I didn't
like. You looked fragile. You looked as though you
had been through the fire of an illness. I hope that
wonderful table of nourishing food that Paula puts
on will soon give you a few more pounds.
I called up Sandy to let her know about the program, got Sandy herself this time over the phone
instead of Charlene, and was pleased to find her
voice so strong and to learn how well she is feeling. Unlike myself and Alice and J.D. she hasn't
quite finished the book, but she said she was having
a wonderful time with it, and marvelled that you
could remember all those things.
Get strong again, come out next year on that program tour. My house is waiting for the boom of
your laughter!

Affectionately,
Lilla

Bring Paula with you.

There was more than one way to keep up with Carl's
doings, as evidenced by the following, written on July 20,
1953:

Dear Carl, --
Someone has just sent me Fanny Butcher's account of your late doings in Chicago. (Clippings
always come to me from all over, every time you
set foot out of Flat Rock. I chuck them into a
bulging manila envelope. Maybe my clipping file is
as bulky as your own.) Anyway Fanny's account was
as good as a letter, tells more than your own letters about you, that you're making a continuation
of the autobiography, working on the one volume
Lincoln, and in the intervals of harder work playing

137

with your poetic fantasies, the Yellow Paper Horse et al.

Among that batch of papers which you sometimes try out on us is the one about the squirrels, "Wither goest thou?" I have dubbed it "The Collectors," and when I pull it out of my purse and read it to any one of my collector groups I always get a laugh. They recognize it.

We are all sorry about last January, but I understand we are to have you this coming one. Your place in this domicile is always ready for you. Why don't you induce Paula to come with you this time? Room for her, too, you know.

If I run over one page you probably wouldn't read it. So I'm signing off.

> My best to all the Sandburg family,
> Lilla Perry

This one other Gerro Nelson bit has turned up among my papers. I have tried to trace her, but no success as yet. This last isn't up to the other verse. She was about fourteen when she wrote it.

Simpleton

I could love a simpleton
　If he were very kind,
And had no reason to obscure
　The level of my mind.

I could love a simpleton
　If he were pacified
With just my heart and nothing more
　Than being by my side.

But, oh, to love a simpleton
　Insistent must I be
That I should be as much
　A silly simpleton as he.

This last stirred a response from Carl on August 17, and he thanked me for a fine letter, and for another Gerro Nelson poem, which he liked. He regarded her as an enigma, with many concealed powers. He wouldn't be at all astonished to see her found one day, but if so, she would be fickleminded, fat, self-satisfied, and an enjoyer of misanthropic wit, the early inspiration gone. Mary has had a second stroke, but recovered from it rather well. Catherine McCarthy was vacationing in California, and planning to visit the Harcourts; might look up me. I should tell her about the diary. He hoped that peace would be with me, and profound good fortune as always.

I did not write Carl again until January 2, 1954, when he was due shortly for another lecture appearance.

Dear Carl,--
Before the month is out we see you! A long year of postponement. The Parnes are in Europe. A day or so ago the Swedish American Central Committee called me up, and wanted to know what they could do to welcome you when you appear. They seemed to want a gathering or reception for you before your program, perhaps for the publicity because you have the largest auditorium in town to fill. I told them, of course, that this house was open to them, and that I had often had as many as forty people here, but they would have to get in touch with you. They said they would reach your agent in New York at once.

I phoned Mary and talked with the family, learning that Mary has made a fine come-back and seemed to be much like her old self. This was just before Christmas.

A fine letter came from Kenneth Dodson, announcing the date his book is to come out, and telling me all that you had done for him. He is already up to his ears in another.

A few days ago came A Lincoln Preface, with Catherine McCarthy's card inside. I looked up your last letter and found that you had told me she was coming to the Coast on her vacation to see the Harcourts in Santa Barbara, and that she might look in on me. I flew to New York to be with Bea about that time, and may have missed her. Anyway I wrote her the best note I could contrive, thanking her for the Lincoln Preface, which I had read the first night it arrived and enjoyed. I took occasion to tell her that I had complete Sandburgiana, I believe, except the text of your book on Steichen. (You were able to get me the photographs.) I have Caswell on the lookout for it. He got me some copies of Poetry, in which some of your earliest things were published.

139

I've turned off quite a task this past year. I organized the old journals and letters, reduced them to ashes, and they now exist in the form of 1823 typewritten pages plus the 311 previously typed out from an earlier period in which I changed the names. Quite a mass of material (four boxes full) to sometime hand over to the New York Public for their archives. You can see I've had a busy year!

My best to all of you, Paula, Margaret, Janet, Helga and yourself,
Lilla

Chapter XVII

Carl Sandburg came and went. He was here from January 26 to February 7. His program at the Philharmonic Auditorium was on January 30. I continued to hear from the Swedish American Society all during January.

"We understand," said Mr. Ederk Fahlstrom, the chairman, "that Carl Sandburg always stays at your home. Have you any idea when he will arrive, Mrs. Perry?"

"I never know when Mr. Sandburg arrives until he phones me from the airport that he is here, or wires me when on his way. But I have never known him to fail an appointment for a program."

"The Swedish American Society would like to further the publicity for his program by putting on a reception for him a day or two in advance. Do you think that could be managed?"

"Knowing Mr. Sandburg well I don't think that it could," I answered. "He usually keeps in seclusion until the date of his program. Your best chance would be to do something for him right after his program. Then he is keyed up at the sight of old friends, and glad to ask them to come to the house afterward. There have been spontaneous gatherings here at my house after all of his programs, and I would be glad to have the Swedish American Society have their reception for him here if they would like it. It is hard to arrange anything in advance for Mr. Sandburg, but it is easy to catch him here for a gathering after his program. How many would there be, Mr. Fahlstrom?"

141

When he told me thirty or forty people I told him we had often had that number. And so it was arranged.

With the town plastered with publicity about his coming, my phone began to ring. When was he due to arrive? When I declared I never knew in advance they hardly believed me. There were his own friends calling, the Swedish American Society, even my son, Caswell, who wanted to know if there was any way in which his friend, Jack Reynolds, the bookman, could meet Sandburg.

"Caswell, my dear, Carl has been coming here all these years because I never ask anything of him. To meet some new person who may mean nothing to him, well, you know, he can be rather ruthless at times."

Then a solution came to me which would solve simultaneously the problem of my own dinner engagement the night of his arrival. I had thought I must break it. "How about your meeting him with Reynolds at the airport, just you two? Carl's a man's man. He would expand more with just you two men. The first word I hear from him, telegram or otherwise, I'll call you, and you can keep in touch with Reynolds."

The plan pleased both my son and his friend. Reynolds hoped Carl would be coming in at International Airport instead of at Burbank, so that the ride with him would be longer.

On my return from my own engagement the night of Carl's arrival the house was all lit up, and Carl, my sister Alice, Caswell, and his friend, were enjoying the laughter and hilarity that Carl always brings with him.

The days before his program were all much the usual pattern. Carl did not appear for breakfast until nearly noon. He was full of good talk, as always. To keep him eating busily while his food was hot, I read him bits from my journal.

I read him my summary of the Charles Lummis letters to his wife, which reveals such a strange story. He seemed to enjoy the account of my visit to Dr. Mary Walker when I was just out of college. Walker was the feminist who made herself notorious by the fact that she was the first woman to wear trousers. I had spent a week on her farm. One morning I asked if he would like to hear about one of my love affairs, and read him the Meredith Armistead Johnston story, which happened during my School of Journalism days. (As I look at what I have written, "love affair," I realize what a different connotation that expression had in Carl's youth and mine. We applied it to the most innocent flirtation. Today it seems to mean something quite different. I can find no expression that would accurately describe the brief adventurous infatuation that was my story.) There were bits I read that pictured the life that went on in this house when the children were young.

Carl seemed to enjoy my selections from the journal, as always, and repeated one of the comments he had made in a recent letter: "That story of yours will have an importance in years to come when the best-sellers of today are dead and gone."

From Tuesday to the night of his concert on Saturday I had to fend off the telephoners. Even to the chairman of the committee that was putting on his program I had to say, "I have talked with Mr. Sandburg. He will be in Los Angeles Friday night."

"On what plane is he due? Can't we send a delegation to the airport to meet him?"

"He is expecting my son, who is the librarian at Burbank, to meet him."

Saturday morning I relieved the minds of Mr. Anderson and Mr. Fahlstrom by letting them know that Carl Sandburg was in town, under my roof. The Philharmonic Auditorium, they told me, had been sold out. They had considerable at stake.

At his program that night it was obvious that his audience loved Sandburg. After his introduction by Edgar Bergen, when he walked onto the stage from the wings, that great audience rose to its feet. It was very moving. I doubt if there was an empty seat in the house.

To me the program was saddening. The rich sonorous voice of his early days that I had known, was gone. People loved him as they will an old actor or actress, for what he had been. His talk, a mixture of comments, anecdotes, and readings from his poems, was without cohesion or plan. The

143

singing of two old folk songs at the finish was pathetic. Carl was seventy-six. The people--"The People, Yes"--of whom he had sung, loved him, they laughed at his sallies, they applauded him, they filled this great hall to hear him, but I wanted to say, "Carl, let this be the last time. Do not try for it ever again."

But he said to me during his visit, "I never think of myself as an old man. I never call myself an old man. I find myself younger than many people half my age."

Somewhere in that audience sat Theresa Anawalt, as old as himself, who had found herself in his autobiography, Always the Young Strangers. What a surprise and thrill it must have given her to find her name there. For he had written in his book about their daily meetings on the sidewalk near St. Patrick's Church--he on his morning milk route, and she on her way to her job in a Main Street store. He had admired her walk and the way she held her head and shoulders as they approached each other at about eight o'clock every morning. As they got closer together he would admire the beauty of her face. After fifty such encounters he began to speculate on what he might say to her by way of greeting, but after consideration, he felt he should leave it to her to speak first. It was not love at first sight or after the hundredth encounter; it was just that he found it wonderful to look at her, an enigmatically attractive girl. They never spoke, then or afterward, nor did he ever hear about her since that time, but he never forgot her.

Theresa Anawalt had found these paragraphs and she had written Carl through his publishers from an address in Glendale, California. She was now married. Doubtless she told him something of her life in the intervening years. I wish I had questioned him more specifically, for the story pleased me. At his program she had sent a little note back stage to him.

> You'd better be good! I'm here in the eleventh row, aisle seat, with ears and eyes alert. I'll come back and see you after the program and when we look at each other after all these years we'll say, "Well, here we are again!"

It was partly that I might catch a glimpse of her that I watched Carl from the outer fringes of the crowd that thronged back stage to see him, to meet him after the program. But Carl told me later that she did not come. When he traced her later over the phone to her Glendale address she made the excuse that there had been too many people. Perhaps with an elderly woman's pride she preferred that he remember her as he had pictured her.

As we came out the stage entrance onto the street I was walking with Carl and had his arm. A beautiful tall elderly woman stood just at the corner of the alley near where we turned into Fifth Street. Her face was lit up with an almost ecstatic smile as though she had just been through a moving experience. As we turned he was at her side and I saw her reach out and touch his arm, so lightly that he did not even feel it. I turned back to look at her, and for a moment we held each other's eyes. She was smiling but there were tears on her face. Up till this moment I have thought of it as a separate incident. As I write this I wonder if it might not have been Theresa Anawalt.

When we reached home there was already a houseful of people there, the Swedish American Society and friends whom Carl and I had asked. My daughter Dorothy had arrived early to take my place as hostess. A refreshment committee of the Swedish society had taken over and I had been warned that I was to have nothing to do with the refreshments. Eleanor Remick Warren, the composer, had brought a singer with her to have Carl hear songs she had written to some of his poetry. Young, tawny-haired William Clauson, whose guitar had been loaned to Carl for his program, sang us a group of Swedish folk songs. He had a fine, well-trained voice, was a young Segovia of a guitarist, and had a strong dramatic sense in his folk-song rendering that woke up the whole party. He delighted Carl so much that he, too, reached for the guitar again and sang to us.

A prominent preacher of the city was among the guests. In my talk with him I learned that he had come in the hope of inducing Carl to speak at a young peoples' group at his church the next morning. I knew the party tonight would last late, the meeting next morning was at nine-thirty. He was asking a good deal of an elderly man, I thought, even if Carl's contract with his agent would permit it. I watched with interest to see what would happen. Carl had seated himself among a group of people. In a brief interval when his attention was not engaged, the preacher strode toward him, bent over him and put forward his request. I saw Carl look upward, fire him an unadorned "No," then turn immediately to the person beside him in conversation.

145

By one-thirty most of the large group had left, but the folksingers were having too good a time to leave. About twelve gathered in the music room, some of them sitting on the floor at Carl's feet, and young Clauson's guitar was handed from one to another until three-thirty. Carl contributed his part as much as anyone. Young Clauson was easily the star performer with his endless repertory and his dramatic fervor. I didn't have to worry about Carl and his fatigue. He had as many defenses as anyone I know. If those young people stayed on it was because he wanted them to.

When the last of the guests had departed all of us were suddenly aware that we were hungry. Mary Keller (who was staying all night with us), my daughter Dorothy, my sister Alice, Carl, and I gathered in the kitchen and ate up the last of the plentiful refreshments. Mr. Metzgar had long since disappeared.

It was quarter past four. "I'll help you make up your couch in the music room," said my sister wearily.

"Go on to bed. I'm not even going to fully undress. All I want is a bathrobe, a pillow and a blanket!" And so it was that I slept until there was a late stirring of my guests in the morning.

Long before Carl made his appearance at one o'clock there came a call over the phone to me. Young Clauson's father told me what a thrill it had given his son to have Mr. Sandburg use his guitar and to have such outspoken approval from him of his singing of the folk songs. Bill was too shy to speak up for himself, but did I think that Mr. Sandburg would be willing to see his father and let him ask for any short statement in writing that Bill could use in his publicity. The young man had had many years of training both of his voice and his guitar playing. He was having a bit of a struggle at twenty-three to get his start.

Knowing Carl and his dislike of meeting people unknown to him, I suggested that perhaps I could do more about getting a statement from him than his father could. "I am sure that you could," was his reply.

I added that we all had been sufficiently impressed with his son's performance to make the effort to get a statement from Mr. Sandburg.

I reported our conversation to Alice, Mary Keller, and

146

Dorothy. They were keen about my getting a word in writing from Carl that would be a help to the young man. I groaned, however, remembering all the work Carl had confided he had before him while staying with us. I had often suspected that there were hours of work behind Carl before he appeared at twelve or one for breakfast. When he spoke once of using powdered coffee in his room I was sure of it.

He had to finish the careful reading of Kenneth Dodson's 508-page book Away All Boats.

He had to write a review of it for the New York Herald Tribune, which must be the best thing of its kind that he had ever done.

He had to contribute "words" that were to be inscribed in bronze over the door of a Swedish hospital. "When they are to be in bronze, you know," he laughed, "it's easier to write a book!"

He was to give a talk on his way home at a new Chicago school, which was to be called the "Carl Sandburg High School."

There was plenty to be done while here to account for his fending off people or any new problems. Yet we wanted that word for young Bill Clauson.

"Perhaps if we worked out a statement ourselves, something we know he would be willing to sign, it might make it easier," suggested Alice. Alice, Mary Keller and Dorothy got into a huddle on the front porch. What they evolved was good, but it didn't sound like Carl. I had to whittle it from that angle. Nothing was satisfactory.

Mr. Metzgar and I had an errand in Pasadena that afternoon. It was a beautiful day, and Carl asked if he could come along for the ride. As I started up my car Alice gave me an appealing look. I might have answered her that I didn't intend to try for anything on that ride. But when midway on our trip Carl burst out in enthusiastic comments on young Clauson's performances of the night before I seized my chance.

"The boy has had lots of good preparation and he's now all ready to go. If you would just write out one statement of the opinions about him you have been expressing, he could

147

use it in his publicity, and it would be of immense help to him. "

"I'll do it, " said Carl.   He tore off the margin of the newspaper he had in his hand, and began to write.   When he handed it to me I was surprised and pleased.   In it he had said much more than we would have dared invent for him. It read:

"William Clauson is a Viking of song, to me irresistible, one of the most colorful and versatile singers and accomplished guitarists I have ever heard. "

When we reached home and showed it to the girls I put a white card in Carl's hand and said, "Don't you want to copy that in more permanent form?"   "Aw no, I done writ' enough, " he drawled.   "Type it out if you like and I'll sign it. "   "We'll give Bill this, as is, " I answered.   I wanted Clauson to have it all in Carl's own writing.   So it was the newspaper margin note that Bill Clauson got.

"Paste it onto something, " I suggested.

"I'll get it photostated at once, " he beamed.

Carl's stay this time had lasted twelve days.   To the people who called up before his program--he had not arrived; to those who called afterward--he had already left town.   I was used to being this buffer.   Many of the people insistent on seeing him were from the press.

"Why should I be interviewed?" he protested.   "I had enough of that sort of thing in Chicago at my birthday celebration.   What do they think I am, a prophet, an elder statesman?   Should I know whether we are likely to be attacked by atomic bombs?   Who do I think is the most promising young writer in America today?   Have I got to decide that?   Jesus wept!" he exploded.

He did consent to letting Mildred Norton of the Herald Express come out to the house.   She had written a report of his program that he liked.   Instead of the walk he had suggested to her when she arrived she took him up into the hills in her car and they walked there.   He came home all enthusiastic about her, her fine mind, her penetrating intelligence.   He did not mention her beauty.

148

He had invited Norton to have dinner with him some-where on the night I told him I had an engagement elsewhere.

"I hate a restaurant!" he commented. (Didn't I know it? Hadn't I had to get dinner for him here at the house every night--I who had forgotten how to cook?) "It would be so much nicer if we could find a place where we could find cheeses, cold cuts, and salads, and could eat them right on your kitchen table."

"Why don't you?" I laughed. "The coast will be clear, everybody out of your way."

"We could sit there and talk, annoyed by no autograph hunters," he added. But in a few minutes an unpleasant thought crossed his mind. "But we'd have to clear it up. I couldn't ask Miss Norton to wash dishes."

"Leave your table just as it is. It won't take me a minute when I get home. You need not tell her that I will do it. Just make a sweeping gesture when you get ready to leave the kitchen and say, 'This will all be taken care of!'"

"You are certainly a good sport," he chuckled.

When I reached home from my evening's engagement I thought Norton would be gone, but I could hear their voices in the lighted kitchen. For a moment I swung open the kitch-en door to laugh at them and to greet her: "Did you ever have a man take you out to dinner this way before?"

"No, I never did," she smiled, "but it's fun!"

I retreated up into the living room of my sister's suite, now given over to Carl. I found Alice there, reading. We were both getting in every minute we could on Kenneth Dodson's book Away All Boats. Alice had gone there to find Carl's advance copy. I, too, had just received an advance copy. We read until Carl himself appeared, Miss Norton having departed.

"You won't need to go near the kitchen," he announced. "It's completely shipshape. Miss Norton insisted on doing the dishes and I wiped them!"

"Carl, it's the first time in my life that I knew you could wipe dishes!"

149

We were all now reading Kenneth Dodson's book, discussing it whenever Alice, Carl, and I got together. Carl had begun his laborious review. I have always felt there is a certain timing element in acknowledging the gift of an authors book. So on February 4 I wrote:

> Dear Kenneth Dodson, --
> I got your book, but Carl Sandburg is still here, so you will know how much time I have to write!
> My sister and I are each picking it up whenever the other lays it down, and Carl has been shutting himself up in his room to work on that review which he is determined shall have carrying power. He wants to make a good launching of that first boat of yours.
> I have a strange feeling as I read. Here I was tucking you up to rest that day long ago when you were here, as though you were a tired little boy. Now I am wondering how a single human being can live and have concentrated on himself so much age-old experience, and with it all that rare awareness that intensifies both joy and agony.
> More anon. You know how it is. I have to feed Carl here at the house. He abominates restaurants. We began with prime-rib roast, now we are down to hash. How much lower can we go? I burnt up a roast yesterday because I was listening to him talk!
>
> Yours gratefully,
> Lilla Perry

Carl sat at breakfast one morning, announcing that his review was almost finished. Just then a telegram was delivered from the editor of the New York Herald Tribune. It was to the effect that since Dodson's book had been dedicated to Sandburg, and his blurb was on the dust cover, they had decided he could not be considered an impartial person to review the book.

"They are late in deciding this," he said with a laugh and with seemingly no animus over the matter. "They knew of the dedication of the book and the blurb when they asked me to review the book. I want very much to help that boy, Dodson. I have faith in the good job he has done. He has found a place in my heart that I have never expected that any one would take. (I wondered if he was thinking of the son

150

he had never had.) There will be other places for that review."

Next morning at breakfast he handed me the typed sheets of his review. I read it through carefully.

"What do you think of it?" he asked.

"Do you want my real reaction to this?" I asked. "Carl, there are people who write books in this world, and there are people who can't write books who write reviews. You have written the books. What you have here is good, the spots you have chosen to quote are telling, but your organization of your material isn't good."

"Go on," he said. "I'm punch-drunk on the thing. I've reorganized it three times. Take it to your typewriter and edit the thing. You are like Catherine McCarthy." He was referring to the editor at Harcourt Brace whom he has always wanted me to meet. "She came down to Flat Rock and worked a week on the one-volume Lincoln with me, helping me with the condensation and the new inserts. To write that new one-volume edition I had to go through all the basic material again, and so much has been discovered since my six volumes were written that there had to be forty inserts." Then he let out his blockbuster laugh at something he was remembering. "One day I inserted a Lincoln story that I knew she would pounce on and cut: 'After Lincoln's telling one of his stories one day a friend said to him, "Abe, there ought to be a collection made of all these good stories you get off, and a book made of them." Lincoln looked at his friend with a twinkle in his eye. "There never will," said he. "They'd stink like seventeen privies!"' Carl said when her pencil cut that one, he roared.

We talked of many other things but when he put on his cap after breakfast to go for his walk he had changed his mind about the review. "I'll be darned if I'll let you touch that review. It's something special. It was gestated in my womb, not in yours. How about giving it a good typing. You said you would."

"I'll be darned if I'll type a review for you that I don't like! Get my sister to do it. She's a good typist."

He called up his nephew, Eric, before he left the house and arranged to have him call for him and take him to his sister Mary's that evening.   Perhaps he was the least bit miffed at me.

Alice typed the review for him next day in her beautiful, perfect typing.   She is a good critic.   She felt the same way about it that I did.   But my one fruitless burst of expostulation had been enough.   She kept what she thought to herself.

On the Friday afternoon before he left at his request I called Paul Jordan Smith, who came bounding over to see him.   Paul was the book editor for the Los Angeles Times. The Times has an enormous circulation.   Carl thought it might reach many people if he gave it to Paul for his paper. Paul seized at the chance to publish it.   "Of course, the Times would be glad to have it.   But you will have to give me a note with your signature to it that it is your review, and you want me to use it."

Carl wrote a humorously worded note to that effect, adding that it was not to be curtailed, mutilated, or dismembered.   If the Times took it, it must go in as written.   Paul was sure there would be no trouble about that.   It was not to be an exclusive.   Carl had other papers in which he intended to place it, one of them a Chicago paper, I remember.

Sometime during these last few days there had been a phone call from New York City wanting him for a television show in Chicago on the evening of Lincoln's birthday, the twelfth, for a reading of his Lincoln Preface.   The fee was to be five thousand dollars.

"The Preface is already written, the reading of it will take about twenty minutes.   Such a fee is fantastic!" was Carl's comment to me when he left the phone.

"Never mind.   What did Marlene Dietrich get at a night club in Las Vegas last week?"

On Saturday, the last day of his stay, Mr. Fahlstrom and Mr. Anderson of the Swedish American Committee called to ask Carl, my sister Alice, and myself to go with them to a Swedish smorgasbord.   It was a small place, and not well known.   In fact, we would have it almost to ourselves, they told us.

"Sounds good to me.   Let's go," said Carl.

There were only seven of us at the dinner. The food was good, the talk was good, and Carl was in one of his most amusing and entertaining moods. The Swedish woman who owned the place fluttered anxiously around, excited at having so distinguished a guest.

Two other patrons, a father and his young son, lingered long at their table, delaying their departure as long as they reasonably could. The young boy's face was beaming. He had probably learned Carl's poems in high school, or "The Fog," at any rate. He had recognized Carl's much-pictured face, and was now actually within earshot of the great man's stories. As they left the room, emptied now of all save ourselves, the boy stood for a moment shyly beside Carl's chair. When Carl looked up he held out a card and asked for his autograph. "There are times when I have to say, 'I'm not working tonight,'" Carl replied. And the boy moved off looking crestfallen. Carl hadn't seen the boy's face as he sat at the table. If he had he would have answered differently.

We had been talking about the Lincoln Preface to be read on the twelfth. "Have you timed yourself on the reading of it?" I asked.

"No, I haven't. Might be a good time to do so right now, if you would all like to hear it," he said.

We moved away to a cleared table and he read the Preface to us.

I used to say Carl could read from the telephone directory and make it interesting, the tricks he plays with vowel sounds and intonations. So it was now. I liked the Preface. There seemed greatness in it.

It was late when we left, everyone in a glow over a fine evening.

Once home again, Carl and Alice and I said our goodnights. I wanted more of Away All Boats before I turned in for the night. So I stretched out on the living-room couch for an hour or so of reading. I had not been buried long in my book when Carl came down the stairs.

"Eric calls for me in the morning at ten-thirty," he said. "I'll have a little time with my sister, Mary, and they

153

will put me on my plane. If I am not down to breakfast by
ten--call me then. I still have a leftover swiftness from my
fire station days, and I'll be down in ten minutes after I'm
called. I'm already packed up," he added.

He sat down at my feet on the couch, and there still
seemed many things to say, after all our days of talk.
Paula's name came in more frequently than it ever did. Once
after my first meeting with Paula I had berated him for never
mentioning what a beautiful, wonderful wife he had. "What
should a feller do, holler about it?" he had answered. I
remembered that as he talked of her now. Once before during his visit he had been telling how changed his life would
have been if, in his early days, he had fallen for a well-
paying job. "Perhaps I wouldn't have written, and as things
would have turned out--I would never have met Paula." It
was as if he rated them as equal calamities and I am sure
that he did.

It was twelve when he rose to go. It was our real
parting. In the morning we knew things would move swiftly.
And they did. There was a quick breakfast in the kitchen,
with Alice putting up sandwiches lest he find nothing to eat
in his friend's empty apartment in Chicago to which he was
to go. Eric came for him. We checked that he had overcoat, bag, carved Japanese cane that I had given him, and
his cap. Mr. Metzgar, Alice, and I stood on the porch and
waved him off.

Next day (February 8) I sent off this note to him, with
a picture of two bear cubs on their hind legs, snarling at
each other, clipped from the day's Times.

> Dear Carl, --
> Some one took this snapshot of us while we were
> yapping over that review.
> And while we were swapping quotations the other
> day, I should have handed you this one: "I would
> rather be a nettle in the side of my friend than a
> mush of concession."
>
> Yours, as always,
> Lilla

But disputation over reviews was the farthest thing
from what Carl wanted to talk about, when he wrote me
shortly afterward an undated, handwritten note on four cards.

Sometime during his visit we must have talked about the technique of printing music and words in connection with his new American Songbag; a matter that had been of some concern to me when I was illustrating the text of my book on piano pedagogy with musical examples. Carl knew enough about the technology of printing to insist in his note that the use of line-cuts or zincs was the solution. He had enjoyed a fine visit and hated to leave. He also appreciated the gift of a Hokusai print.

Chapter XVIII

I continued to toss the correspondence ball during 1954 and 1955. On April 7, 1954, I replied to his handwritten note as follows:

Dear Carl, --

I am glad Kenneth Dodson is refusing to sign a movie contract that would release all his control of what they might do with a picture. They are capable of making a mess of it, as we know. We watch it on the best seller lists, and K.D. attributes it all to the sendoff you gave it.

Caswell is keeping watch of book lists to finish out my Sandburg shelf. A few days ago he made me a present of a Grabhorn limited edition of Bronze Wood, which I had never seen or read before. It is good reading, and I am more than ever assured that you were a wood carver yourself in some previous life that has now become "phantom." My Cornhuskers had been carried around so long under Richard's arm years ago that it was in tatters. This he [Caswell] has replaced, but not the nice inscription of long ago. And since he intended to keep the worn out book himself he would not let me tear it out. So the new copy awaits your pen when you come again. Someday he will run into the Steichen biography and get it for me.

I enclose a crumpled clipping. The press called me up for a verification or denial of your suicide. I wasn't even troubled. I told them you enjoyed life too much for that and assured them they would find it to be a mistake.

Bill Clauson says all his good luck stems from

our party. There he met Eleanor Remick Warren, through her Richard Crooks and others, through them a sponsor for his New York debut in the fall, and a series of concerts in Sweden in the meanwhile. He now has Segovia's autograph under yours on his guitar.

Much more to chatter about. But I learned from you long ago to make a letter a one page affair.

Thanks for the note about the music printing. Rhys Williams, the man whose books on Russia you said you had, writes me that he is to be in your vicinity soon and may have the temerity to call. If he appears during your off-work hours you would enjoy him. He is a real human being, with a sense of humor to match your own.

My best to all at Connemara Farms,

Yours,
Lilla

Six months later I wrote Carl again, on October 6.

Dear Carl, --

That was a fine visit over television last night. My sturdy little houseworker, Dorothy, came running downstairs to tell me you were on. Paula looked well, but little Paula! What a surprise! How she has grown, and what a lovely flower she is!

Your new book arrived more than a week ago, but I already had a chance to read 150 pages of it. About three weeks ago, Caswell phoned me from his library in Burbank and said he was passing my door at six o'clock the next morning, going to San Diego on a book buying binge. He would be busy every minute for two days while down there, but if I wanted to go, and could amuse myself! Did I? Could I? I was out on the porch waiting for him at six. We talked all the way down and back, but except to see him operate in an enormous room lined from floor to ceiling with second hand books, I saw nothing of him. Wahrenbrocks had an advance copy of your new Lincoln, which I immediately borrowed and took off to my hotel room that night. Got a good start on it, and like it immensely. No reviews are out yet, but up in San Francisco last week with the Metzgars, I saw one book store with the entire window built up with a hundred or more copies of the new Lincoln. Irving Stone is boasting that he got a fine letter from you about Love Is Eternal. I wonder. I have skimmed that book and am now going back to your Mary Todd, though Mrs. George Seaton has my copy at the present moment. His book has driven a number of people back to rereading yours.

Did I tell you the Ladies Home Journal wrote me in May that they liked my Music pedagogy book and were having a member of their staff reduce the chapters to articles to run serially in the Journal. They would be submitted to me for my approval first, of course. This letter was signed by their managing editor, but not one word have I heard since. Someday I may have to frame the letter showing the nearest I ever got to publication!

Three people called me up about the television show. It was good! William Clauson, the folk-song singer to whom you gave a boost, has just given a program in Town Hall, and the New York music critics have given him fine reviews. They are a ruthless lot, too.

I'm coming on for a visit to Bea in May. Many thanks for the book. J.D. was delighted with his, too.

Yours,
Lilla P.

Another letter to Carl was inspired by the one-volume Lincoln, as of November 8.

Dear Carl, --

I am more than half way through my Lincoln book; it can't be read fast, you know. Last night I came to that lovely passage about the ticking clock, and recognized it as something you gave to us on your last program at the Philharmonic. I have twice come across a new word that you have coined: "addedly." You can see I am doing no skipping. The book goes to bed with me every night, no matter how long the day. For a while J.D. and I kept about even, but he finally outstripped me, and has finished the book. We used to discuss it at breakfast, and I could just see you in your corner of my kitchen laughing at us.

Not one word from the Ladies Home Journal
since they wrote me last May that they were going
to condense the chapters of my music pedagogy book
into a series of articles and publish it, in fact, they
told me it was being done! I have decided it must
be hell to be a writer!

J.D., after his serious operation of a year or
more ago, is as peppy as ever, and needs restrain-
ing at times. Just recently I caught him up on my
garage roof on a shaky old ladder almost as old as
himself, sawing off a limb of a tree! What I had
to say to him gave our porch-rocking neighbors next
door a good laugh.

Remember me to the girls, and to Mrs. Sandburg. I have fond remembrances of my days at
Connemara farms.

Yours,
Lilla

My next letter was virtually a postscript to the above,
written on November 23, 1954:

Dear Carl, --
Now that I have finished the Lincoln book I won't
be pestering you with letters. I came to the end
of it last night, and read it with tears. You made
us so dearly love the man! I have a suspicion that
you yourself were not without tears when you wrote
that ending. It is a fine and wonderful book, Carl.

Yours,
Lilla.

In the spring of 1955 Harcourt shipped me a copy of
Carl's latest, Prairie Town Boy, a juvenile and much-
shortened version of Always the Young Strangers. I gave
him my prompt reaction in a letter of March 23.

Dear Carl, --
Prairie Town Boy came yesterday, and I read it
all through last evening. I missed some things I
had liked in Always the Young Strangers, but on the
whole, you, as a person, came through much more
sharply than in the earlier book. I loved your description of your walk with the girl on page 137. It
reminded me a little of a writing of my own that I

159

came across recently that I had called, "Do You
Remember Your First Beau?" Probably if you were
here I would get you to eat your breakfast before it
got stone cold by bringing it out opposite your kitch-
en corner and reading it to you. Alice and I got
some laughs out of it, so perhaps I'll send it along
anyway.

The reason I happened to find it was because I
was going through a box of short stories written
over the years to see if I could find any that would
reduce to 1500 word short-shorts. Writers' Digest
announces a contest with 200 prizes, and with such
a big bull's eye I thought I would have a try at it.
This one I'm sending on I can't seem to cut down.
Of course, it is quite ridiculous of me at my age
to still want to see myself in print. If one has gotten there earlier, it is a different matter, one can
keep on, but to try to get published for the first
time at seventy is silly. Count it among my other
amusements, like playing the piano for two hours
every day and fooling around with netsukes and snuff-
bottles!

I hope Prairie Town Boy means that you are going on to later periods. Do you remember after
Prairie Years people used to say, "Of course he
did a wonderful job, he lived the prairie years himself. But he can never do the War Years!" Now
I'm saying to you I don't believe if you go on that
you will ever be able to do justice to the Paula
story, and it must be a very beautiful one. But
you've got reticences you won't be able to over-ride.

End of page (But thanks for the book, Carl.)

                                        Lilla

Chapter XIX

Sometime in September 1955 I was on one of my frequent visits to New York. I had gone into Harcourt Brace's to talk with Carl's good friend Catherine McCarthy. While in her office a call came through from Flat Rock from Carl. After discussing business matters with him for a few minutes, she said, "There is a friend of yours in the office with me." When Carl learned who it was he said, "Put her on!" When he found that my plans included a brief visit to my son Norman at Auburn Polytechnic Institute in Alabama, he was so warm in his persuasions that I stop at Flat Rock for a visit to the Sandburgs, that I made my decision to do so on the spot.

My trip East had not been by automobile this time. I had flown to New York, my favorite mode of travel forever after. To reach Flat Rock I went by train to Asheville, and there Mrs. Sandburg drove to meet me. On our ride home that afternoon she helped me catch up on family history. Helga, the youngest daughter, I knew, had married the young man who had been Carl's secretary at the time of my last visit. Helga, with little John and Paula, both of them the joy of Carl's life, were living near Washington, and Carl had not seen the children since their departure. She spoke feelingly of the loss they were to the family. Margaret and Janet's lives were the same as I had found them on the previous visit. Mrs. Sandburg now had an efficient manager for the goat farm. I judged that correspondence over the sale of breeding stock was now the main part of her work.

Mrs. Sandburg and I reached the house in time for dinner and I left the following afternoon. I remember we sat at the table long after it had been cleared. Carl had a pile of mail, which he shared with us. There were several batches of poetry sent in by would-be poets. One group of verses had been typed in the beautiful printing you get with a fine electric typewriter. It was on Japanese vellum and between each leaf was a protecting page of tissue.

"This poor lad must have thought very highly of these poems," Carl commented. "And listen to them!" He read one or two of the short pieces. They were utterly without merit or promise.

"Are all the poems you get as bad as that?" I inquired.

"No, many are much better. I told you once that of the tons of verse that have been sent me over the years for my comment I never had received anything as good as Gerro Nelson's."

"Now, what will you do, send these back?"

"If they send me an addressed stamped envelope, Margaret takes care of them for me. But they seldom do that thoughtful thing. If I answered all this mail I would never get any time for my own work. I once thought of writing a sort of form letter to return to them. It would be something like this: 'If you are a real poet, nothing I could say would discourage you. If you are not a poet, nothing I could say would really help you.' I should have done it, I suppose, but I never have."

Later we sat in a cozy little living room. I was glowing over a book that my son Caswell had recently given me, Out of These Roots, by Agnes Meyer, an autobiography by the wife of the owner of the Washington Post. As I went on talking about the book Carl's smile grew wider and wider. "You wouldn't know, of course, that Agnes Meyer is one of our very special friends. She has sat many a time in the corner of that davenport where you are now sitting. I wish I had known you were going to stop in Washington. I would have given you a letter to her. But I might have known you would find her a kindred spirit. Why don't you write her anyway and tell her just what you've been telling us about her book. There is one facet of her character you wouldn't know from the book--she is as hipped on Oriental art as you are. I have another book of hers around here somewhere on Chinese painting."

We sat talking late. I knew, of course, I wouldn't be seeing Carl the next day until just before I left.

I remember Carl and Paula walking down the country lanes with me after lunch the next day to a place on the highway where I took a bus to my train. Carl's talk was a sort of paean of joy to--just living!

"I don't see why with Carl's good health and the good care he is now taking of himself why he should not have ten more active years," Paula said wistfully. "He doesn't work all around the clock any more, doesn't push himself as he used to do. Anyway, if Carl never wrote another book--he's done enough." Paula said this with emphasis.

"I'm not ready to stop yet. The doing things is a good part of my joy of living."

On this pleasant note I left them with a hug from both of them.

Before starting for home I went on to Auburn, Alabama, as planned, to visit Norman and Frances. While there I wrote Carl and Paula the following "bread and butter" letter, on October 10:

> Dear Paula and Carl,--
> There has been a single line which has haunted me most of my life, but I have never found it in any anthology, and have begun to believe that I must have made it up myself. "THERE IS NEVER A TURN IN THE ROAD BUT WE SHALL MEET AND PASS IT." When I was back at 720 planning this trip I said to myself, "There will come a moment when I will be sitting at Bea's piano, playing, and she will come in from the kitchen and question, 'What was that, Mother? What was that you were playing?' There will come another moment when I will have little Billy on the piano stool, teaching him the names of the keys and how to play Happy Birthday, and I'll be feeling nearer to the little fellow than any time in my visit. There will come a time when I will be sitting at Carl's hospitable and bounteous board, and he will reach into his pocket or draw some paper out of a book beside him, saying 'Listen to this. This is a good one!'"
> All these things, and other imagined moments

163

happened,--turns in the road that I have met and passed. In little more than a week now I'll be home, for these two young people, Frances and Norman, live very busy lives, and we can pack into a week as much or more than we could drag out in three. In the intervals of talk Norman has been absorbed in his Lincoln book to which he may make reply with a math thesis of his own.

Thanks for all your kindnesses during my visit.

Lilla

Kenneth Dodson's book Away All Boats went on the best-seller list in April 1954. It remained there for months. When it was made into a film Dodson himself visited in Los Angeles briefly. Our household came to know him well. In fact, some of the time he stayed with us. I found him the sincere, unassuming person Carl must have thoroughly liked. He was an excellent talker. That, too, Carl would have enjoyed. I heard much about the week that Carl had spent with the Dodsons, working with him on that first book. His second book was now well on the way to completion. He and his family were on their way to Honolulu, where they planned to settle for a year on a small island near by. There he would get away from continuous telephone calls and visitors. In his hometown, since his success with his first book, these had been impossible to escape.

Naturally one of my first questions was to ask what the movies had done with his story. He said it was hard to talk about that without losing his temper. They were spending two million and a half on the production. Technically it would probably be fine. But they had twisted and mauled his human story out of all recognition. They had built up the character of Captain Hawks, and made MacDougall, his most sympathetic character, into something of a weakling. He felt the script writer had cheapened the story. Though I could see there was much feeling about it, he was now inclined, after a losing battle, to shrug it all off. They had bought the book and paid for it. He had better not consider it his any more. He would always write sea stories, he thought, because the sea is his great love. He would never want to own or live in any house that lacked a view of the sea.

I asked him when he first got the idea that he wanted to write. He thought it was when he was fourteen or fifteen. But he wanted sea adventure first. When he graduated from a Pasadena high school at seventeen he tried in vain to get himself a job on some boat at the Los Angeles harbor. It was Depression time, and there wasn't a chance. He stowed away in one whose first docking was at San Francisco.

"Didn't they find you?"

"I didn't wait to have them find me. As soon as we were out at sea, I showed myself. I was put to work, but I didn't care about that. When I reached San Francisco I had just two cents in my pocket. I spent it for a stamp, I remember. I roamed the docks, hunting in vain for a ship that would take me on. Then I got hungry. I knew the Salvation Army did things for people who were hungry and I hunted it up. While I stood talking to a man at a window, he reached back of him and took a big wedge of apple pie out of a box. Some bakery used to send their day old pies there, I think. I must have wolfed it down, for he handed me another. Then he fixed me up with some meal tickets and a flophouse to sleep in. It was not too clean a place and there were bedbugs, but what troubled me the most was the snoring of the men around me. It was the loudest snoring I have ever heard.

"There were two captains to whom I constantly reported to try to get a job. Neither one had anything for me. But one of them, I think, got tired of my asking. He wrote a note to the other asking him to give me a place. Now mind you, I had gotten nowhere with him myself but a note from the other captain pulled the trick. He signed me on."

Then he told of the mad scramble to get his things to the boat. He had shaken free of the flophouse by this time and found a small clean room for which he did certain services around the place. Now to get there for his things presented a problem, for he had carfare for only one way. He should have run for it while his hands were empty, but he miscalculated. He went there on a streetcar and then had to walk the two miles to the wharf with his load of luggage.

Until his injuries during the war put an end to it for a time, he followed the sea for twenty-five years.

My sister, Alice, present at one of our breakfast talks, asked him how a man who had come up from the ranks ("through the hawse pipes" he put it) felt about junior officers from colleges all over the country, who knew little of ships

165

or the sea, yet during the war were put over seasoned petty
officers.

He gave a laugh. "I have to hand it to those youngsters. A few of them were impossible, but most had real
potential. They certainly learned their specific duties fast.
Nothing could have taught them so quickly as to be thrown
into the complicated actions of a war. When I was their age
(in peacetime, of course) I could have become an officer two
years before I did, but waited because I felt I did not know
enough. Now, after two years in action, these youngsters
were doing a fine job, but they certainly were dependent upon
those few of us who had the technical training and years of
experience. Nobody can learn all that stuff in two or three
years.

"The commanding officers we had--we got a new one
about once a year--were Annapolis graduates, Classes of
1916, 1922, and 1925. Each man brought a wealth of naval
and technical knowledge to our ship. Yet while these men
taught us old-timers, they also learned from us. It was an
exchange program that helped all of us and helped the ship.
They could be hard taskmasters, but they gave of themselves
night and day, and the ship, for all its little woes, was the
better for them."

I was interested in his saying that they seldom put in
places of high command a man whose I.Q. was more than
135. I wanted very much to know why. Men with a higher
I.Q. had too much imagination, he said, and were likely to
see too many sides to a problem, a fact that hindered split-
second decisions. They were less likely if a wrong decision
were made to be able to shrug it off. Theodore Roosevelt
had once said that a second-best decision fully carried out
was more valuable than a best decision followed through wav-
eringly.

One morning I tried to tell him of the experience I
had had a few days before at the home of George Seaton, the
well-known movie director. Mr. Seaton had shown me an
example of what the Screen Actors' Guild had been doing
about restoring some of the very earliest picture films.

To secure copyright a copy of every film had to be
deposited with the Library of Congress. But there had been
explosions of celluloid and the Library would not accept them
in that form. They received copies of the films in tight

rolls. When these earliest rolls were sent out to the studios from the Library of Congress it was found that they could not be unrolled without destroying the pictures. They had to be shipped back. In returning them one roll was missing, however, and the studio detective was told to find it. He found it all right, but not until he had become thoroughly interested in these deteriorated rolls of celluloid nearly fifty years old, so valuable and yet so useless. He experimented and found an answer that would restore these rolls. A dip in some kind of chemical, then some other kind of bath, and they unrolled, the pictures intact. The film Mr. Seaton threw on the screen showed us a newsreel, a parade in New York City of the first automobiles, Theodore Roosevelt in his early forties, a succession of historically interesting events. What we saw had been photographed from the early pictures. Reproduced on the screen of today the old pictures no longer jerked as the early movies had done. They now ran smoothly. I saw a picture of the specially built machine doing this work. It was the uncovering of a lot of fascinating material; 70,000 feet of film had already been done. There remained about two million and a half. It was to be done by the Screen Actors' Guild as they got the money to do it.

On December 1 I wrote again to the Sandburgs.

    Dear Paula and Carl, --

    I've got to get over an inhibition about writing you letters. It is not easy to realize that, though on principle you don't answer them, a sort of self-preservation principle, yet it is just possible that you might like to get them.

    Since Carl made his pronouncement while pacing back and forth in the dining-room that fifteen minutes of TV was just as remunerative and far less wearing than lecture programs over the country, I have had the feeling that I am not in the future going to have many opportunities to corral Carl at the breakfast table and spin my own yarns to keep Carl's breakfast from congealing on his plate! That's a frightfully packed sentence, but you will understand it.

    What I mean to say is, that some of the yarns I will now have to pass along in letters. I collected a few at Thanksgiving dinner. I didn't have a big dinner here, with a family reunion as I have often had. The family is pretty much scattered now anyway, and "family reunions" were never a joy. I love to be with the members of my family, individually, but when I get them all together they act terribly. Some of the in-laws don't like each other, and my own tribe will tell the most outrageous tales of family doings that never happened, to see the in-laws gasp, I suppose. Some one should write a short story of a family reunion, full of its humor and other ingredients! Then, too, I've cooked, or supervised the cooking of, so many Thanksgiving dinners that it was good to sit down in a good restaurant before a dinner I had had nothing to do with.

We got to talking about embarrassing moments that we had lived through, and it brought out some amusing experiences, I can assure you. I had my own to contribute, but when I got home I remembered another which I hadn't told--because it wasn't much to my credit, perhaps. I ran this one I hadn't told off on the typewriter a few days later, and with it one that Caswell contributed when I told him of the "embarrassed moment" confessional. It is too good not to pass on to you. I only wish I could hear your laugh.

> My best to all at Connemara Farms,
> Lilla

Again, on February 12, 1956, I was impelled to write a note:

Dear Carl, --
Have had you much in mind today because we are to see your face on television tonight.

At long last I did as you suggested, and wrote a note to Agnes Meyer in appreciation of her book. I got such a heart-warming reply from her, so much expressed in five lines:

> I was enchanted with your letter (she wrote) and the picture of you and Carl talking me over. I thank you for giving me such a vivid picture of your conversation and am delighted that my book gave you such pleasure.
> If you are ever in Washington, do come to see me.

> With warm regards,

sincerely yours,
Agnes E. Meyer

The magazines have been telling of the sale of your library, that wonderful library of yours. Somehow I can't imagine your living without that background of books which cover every wall of your house. I hope it only means that eventually, and only when you no longer need them, will the University inherit them.

J.D. a short time ago gave me the latest book on Hokusai. It will soon be on its way to you.

As always,
Lilla

Called Mary about the Ed Sullivan show tonite. They will all be listening.

About the first of January 1957 J.D. passed over to me a humorous little penciled note from Carl to me, which had been enclosed with a letter he had just received from Carl, along with some unnamed articles. The gist of it was that if J.D. didn't let me read the articles in question, I was to appropriate them and lock them up. To this bit of jollification, I replied on January 4:

Dear Carl, --
Yes, J.D. passed over the papers. Also your much appreciated little note. First time I've seen your handwriting for a long time.

You know I'd serve as a pretty good clipping bureau for the Sandburg activities. There isn't much that gets into the papers and magazines that some one doesn't forward it to me. Must run pretty parallel to Margaret's collections of clippings about you. But here is a precious one that might have gotten by you! It would be too bad for you not to see it. So I enclose it--with love to all my Flat Rock friends.

Yours,
Lilla

P.S. Norman is Research Professor of Mathematics now--writing a math text book.

169

On March 16 I wrote Carl a short note on a postcard:

Dear Carl, --
   Have just received from a Chicago friend the
Chicago Sunday Tribune Magazine, in which the article appears which connects Callahan's photographs
with your poems. I like it. It goes into my C.S.
file which must be almost equal to your own. Best
love to all of you at Flat Rock,

Lilla

On May 19, 1957, I became concerned about Kenneth
Dodson and wrote Carl the following:

Dear Carl, --
   Do you ever hear from Kenneth Dodson nowadays?
I don't, and I used to hear quite frequently when he
was over on that island and plugging away on that
second book, Stranger to the Land. I never found
any reviews, good or otherwise when it came out.
It seemed to have sunk out of sight without creating
a ripple. I turned my advance copy over to Mrs.
Seaton, who saw that it reached the right spot for
a movie review. Nothing came of it. He may be
somewhat in the doldrums since his second book
failed to click. Yet that man can write. Break
your rule, my friend, and send him a card. It
would be better than three stiff drinks! (which he
w'd'nt take).

Much love,
Lilla

On June 16 Carl wrote me a note expressing his appreciation for a shirt and cap I had sent him. He had just
re-read the small book on Hokusai I had given him long ago
and still thought it wonderful what that old boy could react
to and get onto paper. He assured me that the Sandburg
family was always thinking of me, and he was wagering that
he would have more than two trips yet to Los Angeles, and
partake of coffee and eggs, prepared by me in that old kitch-
en of fond memories.

In November along came another of Carl's books from
Harcourt, and this I quickly acknowledged on November 12.

Dear Carl, --

You are so generous in sending me your books! The Sandburg Range arrived just a few days ago. As yet I have done no more than go through the table of contents, nibble here and there, and look for things that I would have wanted included in such a sampling. I think it is a wonderful compendium for a younger generation which hasn't read your books as they came along. It will be on the table by the side of my bed for a good while to come.

Paul Jordan Smith's comments on Sandburg Range came out yesterday on the book page of the Times which announced his retirement. Good picture of him, too. I am enclosing it for you.

By the way, the last time I saw Paul he wanted to enlist my persuasion in getting you to come out here to the coast to live as guest at a settlement of younger generation writers and artists. It sounds to like a Peterboro idea and they need a big name and an inspiring personality to give the enterprise flavor. Paul is one of the directors of it. I've been remiss in not writing you about this. I am sure the invitation holds good for anytime that you might want to spare a couple of months from that wonderful setting that you have right there in Flat Rock. Perhaps I felt it couldn't compete and so did not write you about it. Unselfish of me, wasn't it? For we might, thereby, see a little of you.

My Chicago friends make a pretty good clipping bureau of Sandburgiana! You have certainly been getting around lately. My love to the girls and Paula,

> Yours, with warm regards as always,
> Lilla

On January 2, 1958, I sent Carl a copy of Bill Clauson's Town Hall program, and a review of the program in the New York Times of December 16, 1957. Along with these went a brief note:

Dear Carl, --

I am sending this N.Y. Times reviewer's comment on Bill Clauson's program in Town Hall. It is always good to find our opinion justified and Bill feels he owes his first step up the ladder to your few sentences of comment about him which you

allowed him to use. I stopped in to see his Swedish parents recently and they have a good newspaper
print of you framed and on top of their upright piano.

Yours as always,
Lilla

Chapter XX

Although probably less and less inclined to write as time went on, Carl did not forget me, as evidenced by my letter to him of January 12, 1958.

Dear Carl, --
Soon after the two books came, I wrote Catherine McCarthy to ask if she had sent them. Ever since our luncheon together in New York and one or two gracious notes from her since that time, I have thought of her as an old friend, and wouldn't have been too surprised if she had sent them. Her note a day or two ago told me they were from you.

For several hours today I have been absorbed in the Van Doren short stories and found them fascinating and delightful. I wonder why I have never read anything of his before, short stories, I mean. Thanks so much for making me acquainted with them. The titles of the Best Essays look alluring and I shall soon be in the midst of that.

It is as though I belonged to a clipping bureau on anything that you may be doing. Everyone sends me items. I suspect I've seen more publicity than you on the celebration of your 80th birthday. Mary Alice Metzgar sends me everything from the Chicago papers and Beatrice from the New York ones. It hardly seems possible that it is five years since the celebration of your seventy-fifth, when your friends out here met at Jake Zeitlin's book store and carried on very much as your friends in Chicago were doing! Five years goes by too fast at our time of life. I wish we could slow it up a bit!

Among the items sent me was a poem from the

Chicago Sunday Tribune by Olive Carruthers "Portrait of Sandburg." I should have been very proud
if I could have written it. Did you see it?

The clippings all go into one box and someday
you--who have never patronized a clipping bureau--
may be surprised to look them over.

You are not home. You are off on new adventures connected with this 80th birthday celebration,
I know, but remember me fondly to Paula and the
girls. And my best to yourself.

from
Lilla

Ten days later I was inspired to write Carl because
of his having steered an interesting item my way:

Dear Carl,--

Received yesterday a brief note from Mary Zim-
merman, forwarding to me the Columbus Dispatch
magazine with the article she wrote, "Meet the
Rootabaga Special." I laughed heartily over some
of it. I could parallel her impressions of you as
a visitor in so many ways. But if I should really
let myself go, Carl, I could even do better than
she did. Our friendship has an edge on hers in
time, anyway. She did a pretty good job. I note
she also is of the librarian tribe. I thought some
of the pictures exceedingly good.

Thanks a lot for having her send it on to me.
It was almost as good as the shadow of a visit from
you, or as if I had walked in for a brief spell at
Connemara Farms. Anyway, the equivalent of a
three-line note from you.

Do this again when anyone writes up an interview.
For a man who still has a dozen books he wants to
write, it saves the effort of a letter. And I kinder
think we'd better keep in touch. Odd numbers or
even numbers we haven't, in reason (as my Grand-
mother used to say), too many years ahead of us.
Isn't it wonderful to be enjoying with real zest these
later ones. I look around me and I don't see many
people doing it.

My best to Paula and yourself,
Lilla

The following was a letter of condolence upon my
learning of his sister Mary's death, written on August 17.

Dear Carl, --
I was away on a trip to San Francisco at the
time Mary went, saw no Los Angeles papers, and
have only just learned of it through friends who
saw the notices. There is extra paving in Hell for
all the good intentions I had of seeing your sister
oftener than I did. But Mother used to say there
is never a death without regrets--for something.
I am sorry she could not have stayed to live through
the celebration event of September 21. She would
have glowed with pride in you. But we must remember that she had had many years of that. You
are saddened, I know, but I know, too, that you
have a philosophy of life that enables you to take
things as they come. I have not yet talked to Eric
or Charleen. Time rushes on and we shall soon
be seeing you. I found the Harry Golden book here
on my return. Good of you to remember me with
it. I shall get to it very soon.

My love to all of you,
Lilla

In less than two months I had to write to Carl about
another death, this time of someone even closer to me. This
was on October 9.

Dear Carl, --
J.D. died yesterday leaving a great emptiness
in this household after 25 years in it.
I knew he was leaving us when Margaret wrote
but I did not speak of it, fearing it might prevent
her visit if she knew. J.D.'s daughter has been
here for two months and may possibly remain with
us. I hope so. She is taking her father's ashes
back to the little town of Port Byron, on the Mis-
sissippi River where he was born. At his request
there is to be no funeral.
Tell Margaret I am looking forward to her coming. Her visit just at this time will be a great
help to me. It will help me bear a deep aching
sense of loss.

Affectionately,
Lilla

175

Later in October 1958 Paula and Margaret traveled to the Coast. Paula had a convention of the American Milk Goat Record Association to attend in Riverside, so we did not see her. Margaret stayed here several days. They were pleasant but very active days for me, for Margaret was insatiable in her desire to look at my collections. She spent hours over the Japanese netsuke, studying and appreciating each piece. The lacquer inro were new to her and she examined each one as though she herself were a collector. I gave her the key to my Chinese snuff bottle boxes and she went back to them again and again. She did not know the meaning of the casual glance for anything beautiful. There were many pieces that I felt belonged to her more rightfully than they did to me.

On November 23, 1958, came "A Tribute to Carl Sandburg," in Royce Hall at the University of California at Los Angeles. In the interval since I had last seen him Carl's constant appearances on television had made me feel that I had kept in touch. At first he had felt the prices offered him for these television appearances were fantastic. He had so expressed himself to both Catherine McCarthy and myself. Later he made no demurral when his agent asked outrageous fees for him. He came to take them for granted, I believe. A letter of my own, which I find with a brief reply of Paula's, tells of the important event of this visit.

The day after Thanksgiving, 1958
[November 28, 1958]

Dear Paula, --
Carl, as of course you know, is at Norman Corwin's this time. He has deserted me for the first time since 1920, but it is quite forgivable. I drove out to see him the day before yesterday and found him hard at work on some sort of script in a fine little guest house beside a big swimming pool. It must be quite ideally isolated from the household activities, a fine place for getting work done.
Carl had sent me tickets for the show Hollywood put on for him at U.C.L.A. I had gone, wondering whether it would be the kind of thing he would like or would be at all worthy of him. It was wonderful! I doubt if any poet in all history has ever had such a tribute. The big auditorium at the University was packed. Dr. Frank Baxter, the U.S.C. professor who has put Shakespeare and other clas-

sics on programs, was master of ceremonies. In his hands it could hardly go wrong. He sat at a table--just as he does for his programs--and talked off the script which I suspect was Norman Corwin's. But you would never know it was not his own, with his many ad libs.

There was an empty throne-like chair in the center of the stage with Carl's guitar beside it, books piled high at its foot. Carl came in and took this seat to a rising ovation at the start of the program. Grouped across the stage were other empty chairs which were gradually filled as one by one leading actors and actresses of Hollywood came onto the stage, recited or interpreted whichever of Carl's poems had been assigned to them and took their seats. Some of them were thrillingly good, others not. "I am an ancient reluctant conscript," one of my favorites, which I always hear in Carl's own voice, was unsatisfactory. No wonder that did not satisfy me. I had heard Carl read it so often. One could tell when Carl was pleased. He gave the performance a salute.

At the finish came Carl's part. He talked to us a little, sang one folk song, which made us want more, read some new verse, and then it was over. People thronged the stage, of course.

Carl had seen to it that I got an invitation to the party at the Edwin Pauleys' afterward. I knew the family well because I had once taught their children music, and to my surprise there were a lot of other people whom I knew.

When Carl and I were talking it over at Corwin's later I was saying that I wished you could have been there. You have had many occasions of being proud of him, but these young people reciting his poems would have given you a new kind of lift. I said as much to Carl and he said, "Why don't you write Paula about it? You can give her a better idea than I can." (The rascal! I doubt if you hear from him except by phone or wire once he gets away and is caught up by the rest of the world.)

I had driven out to Norman Corwin's because people, expecting Carl to be with me, had been bringing in books to be autographed. Quite a stack of them had collected.

Carl said he would try to get over to see me before he left for home, but he and Corwin seem

to be very busy and I doubt if he manages it.   Tell
Margaret she did not stay half long enough.   There
were fields for her appreciation into which I never
had time to take her.

Yours,
Lilla

Carl's stay at the Norman Corwins' extended over
several weeks.   Together they were working on the script
of what later became The World of Carl Sandburg.   The germ
of that successful bit of theater came surely from the university program where Carl's poems were interpreted by the
people of the moving-picture world.

During those days of work I saw Carl several times.
Once he had Mildred Norton, who was doing some secretarial
work for him at the Corwins', drive him here for the afternoon.   Once Mrs. Corwin phoned and asked me over to dinner.   This was at Carl's instigation, I am sure.   I'm not
certain she was too happy about it, for she was her own
cook.   No matter what the financial means available, a hostess seems to have that role thrust upon her these days.
Good household help is a great rarity.   There was a nurse
for the two children, I observed, who fed them and put them
to bed before our own dinner.   Before Carl came in from
his guesthouse workshop in the garden Mrs. Corwin spoke
quite feelingly, I thought, about Carl's unwillingness to be
taken out to dinners.   I was laughing inside.   Didn't I know!
Dinner was a gay affair, however.   Carl can always make
it so.   I was amused at his calling forth my own funniest
tales.   He was determinedly not being the star on this occasion.

Soon after this dinner party Carl called up to say
goodbye.   He was leaving for home.   Mr. Corwin was driving
him to the airport.

Chapter XXI

On one of the last days of January 1959 Carl Sandburg's velvet voice came over the phone, long distance from New York.

"They are flying me out as a guest on the first trip of the jet plane, four hours and a half from New York. Ain't that somethin'?"

"Be you alookin' fer a home?"

"Yes, we're arriving in Los Angeles at eight-thirty day after tomorrow evening and I'll be seeing you. Four and a half hours now between New York and you! On the base of one of the pillars around here is the inscription 'The Past is Prologue.' Someone asked a taxi driver going by if he knew what that meant. His answer was, 'I reckon it means you ain't seen nothin' yet.'" We both laughed.

"It will be good to be with you and your familiar household again."

"We'll be expecting you."

Our phone talk was over. I was sitting meditating over it when Dorothy, my competent housekeeper, who did everything but cook for us, passed through the room.

"Where shall we put him?" I asked. "He walked across that stage at U.C.L.A. like a man of forty, and perhaps on account of his daily exercises he could still go up two flights to the sun-deck room, the place he used to like on the third floor. But, after all, he is eighty-one. I don't like to put him there this time."

"Why not put him in the guesthouse? He would be its first occupant since it was all fixed up."

We decided it should be the guesthouse in the garden.

I still sat by the phone feeling a trifle depressed. I was realizing unpleasantly that I was old. I hadn't the energy to cope with Carl. Once an endless vitality in me had risen to meet his exciting visits. I remembered the gay moods in which I had once met them. It was the contrast that depressed me. Carl was a stirring, stimulating person and always had been. But now I shrank back from being either stirred or stimulated. It was as though I had had enough of life and were wearied. "We are ready for death when we are like this," I thought sadly. "Well, perhaps I am, and it takes something like his coming to tell me so."

Then, too, even in physical activity his visits were demanding. His noontime breakfasts were nothing, of course, but he hated restaurants and wouldn't be taken out to dinner. I was going to have to cook dinners, I, who had reached a point where, at times, I'd rather go without than fuss with food. Well, I'd tell him frankly that going out to our dinners was an indulgence my sister and I accorded our old age, and he'd just have to come along. I did tell him exactly that the day after his arrival. He answered blithely, "You know there is nothing I like better than to raid a refrigerator. I am really the easiest man in the world to feed. Plenty of milk, fruit, cheese of almost any kind, and occasionally cold cuts of meat, that is all I need."

The jet plane was due at eight-thirty. Mildred Norton phoned me that the plane was late and had been battling headwinds. She was waiting for him at the airport and would bring him to the house, but could not tell just when. She didn't want me to worry. It had been kind of her to phone. As I lay on the couch in the living room waiting for him, I was thinking that he probably never set foot in a hotel.

When he and Mildred arrived about eleven, I suggested that we take his one bag and bulging briefcase out to the guesthouse, where I was going to put him. He had never noticed the guesthouse before. It had always been rented. Tonight I was rather proud of its comforts. My housekeeper had turned on the heat and the lights and the gay red poinsettia at the stone steps keynoted the bright colors of the place. Carl and Mildred were exclamatory over it, and prowled through the dressing room and the newly painted bathroom before we returned to the main house for a talk.

The days of his visit took on the old-time pattern. I was usually busily working on my memorized piano programs when he came in for his late breakfast. Sometimes he would stop by the piano and say, "Go on, go on." At the breakfast table he would talk off the ideas he had for a magazine article on that first trip of the jet plane, or try out on me what he had written the day before. Such an article had been commissioned in advance.

On the first night I served dinner on T.V. trays and invited my friends who lived in the house (though not eating here) who would normally expect to meet my distinguished visitor. Over food Carl finds it easier to be generous of himself to people who are not of his own choosing. It went off well, and I got no beratings, as poor sister Mary had, when she invited in all her neighbors. Perhaps it was because the time given was limited to the time of the dinner. I saw to it that it was.

Late the following afternoon the magazine editor called to go over Carl's article with him. He stayed so late that they strolled out to dinner about seven-thirty. (I, too, had intended we should stroll!) Later Carl told me they found such a nice place within a few blocks up on Wilshire, where they picked up their food cafeteria style and ate on a balcony where they had sat long and talked, quiet and undisturbed. The manager, Carl laughed, had recognized him, however. He came to their table and introduced himself. They had wandered into Manning's Coffee Shop. It had been an empty balcony because they were latecomers. Carl had been quite taken with the place.

Carl, I thought, you had found it reasonable in price and no tipping! Your thrifty attitude toward such things amusingly still holds. Yet when I heard such traits of yours pointed out in criticism by others, I recalled your many compensating qualities. I recalled the time I saw a shabbily dressed man come up to you after one of your programs. You greeted him warmly, asked him quick questions. I asked you later who he was. "A pal of mine in the socialist days. By the way, drive me to your bank, will you? I want to send him a cashier's check. He may guess whom it is from, but his pride will be saved the embarrassment of having to thank me." I remembered he bought a three-figure check.

181

Yes, Carl would like Manning's. Mildred Norton, whom he took there the next night, after she had pounded the typewriter for him all the afternoon, was not so much taken with the place. I knew it from the laughter with which she told me where they had gone to eat.

When not interrupted by other writing Carl was working on the second part of his autobiography, a continuation of Always the Young Strangers. It is to be called Ever the Winds of Chance. I was challenging him to do justice to his love story with Paula. I am sure it must have been a rare and fine one, and Carl was likely to be very reticent about deeply personal things. Many years ago I remember one of my friends saying to him, "But, Mr. Sandburg, you do not write love poems. I thought poets always wrote love poetry!"

"Perhaps I do," he had answered, "but maybe I write them just for myself and don't publish them." He brought me one sometime later, though he never showed it to my guest who had challenged him. Apparently it was complete, finished as he wanted it, but he never put it into any of his published work.

There was reticence here in that he never published this and perhaps others that he did not show me. It made me feel that he would never do justice in his second volume of autobiography to his meeting and his love for Paula. I awaited that new volume with much interest. We were talking of this portion of his story one day when he said, "I think one of the finest love stories I've heard is one you told me at breakfast one day about Norman and his wife, Frances."

I remembered what it was. Visiting them for the first time when my son, Norman, went to teach at San Jose College, I had commented to Frances that she must be glad that in their new abode Norman had a study of his own, with a big desk and tables where all his books and papers could be piled in one room.

Frances looked at me with a puzzled expression. "He doesn't use it much," she answered. "If I am at the piano he brings his papers in and works at the coffee table nearby. If I want to make a cake in our small kitchen he comes and clears a space to work on the end of the kitchen table. He follows me with his papers and books all over the house."

That story seemed to have pleased Carl. "I would

182

have given much in my life to have had a son like Norman,"
he added.

"Even you couldn't always have understood him, Carl.
He would have been a trial often." While we were on the
subject of Norman I dug out some old diary pages I wanted
to read him. In them I included a portion of a letter to
Norman from Frances. It showed the way she had met Norman's being sent home from Officers' Training Camp at Great
Lakes. "Neurosis without psychosis," the report to me had
read. There had been a letter from a doctor at the Training
Center as well. In it he warned me that I would find Norman
in a deeply depressed state of mind and advised my treating
his being sent home as casually as possible. Frances, of
course, had not seen this warning letter yet she had written:

> So they have decided you are a nut! Well, I've
> always known you were a nut, and that's why I love
> you. I like you best as a civilian anyway. Let
> others be naval officers. You stay home and do
> their mathematical computations for them.

Carl read the brief letter through twice (I had it, of
course, because Norman never threw away anything) then
Carl took off his glasses and wiped his eyes.

Carl surprised me next morning by asking if I would
let him have copies of portions of the old journal that I had
read him. I was reluctant. They were so frank, so personal, those sections I had read him. Reading them to him
was different, letting him have the typed sheets to use or
lose was something else again. He saw my reluctance and
was quite visibly hurt or vexed. Next morning I handed him
the pages, tailored a bit in their preface so they could never
be traced. He had so often wanted for himself things I have
read him that I suppose I should have felt pleased.

While talking about Norman I had described the dis-
order in which he left his desk and tables, and still does.
Carl laughed. "I'm the same way myself. Papers and memoranda just pile up in my workroom and I won't let anybody
touch them. I never destroy anything. My manuscripts will
all go to the University of Illinois. They have a Sandburg
room there. I have sometimes thought of stuffing all my
loose papers and memoranda into envelopes and turning them
in also. What a wonderful thing it would have been for me
when I was writing my Lincoln books if the notations made
at Lincoln's desk had been saved."

Then that visit, too, was over. A few days later, February 12, 1959, we all watched television while Carl gave his Lincoln talk before the joint session of Congress. The place was packed with dignitaries from all nations. All rose when Carl's turn came on that Lincoln memorial program. A storm of applause greeted its close.

More than once during his visit Carl had spoken of his wish to invite his grandchildren, little Paula and John, to hear him give his talk before Congress. He could get them seats for the Congressional meeting, but he feared, he said, it would look as if he wanted them to see him under exalted circumstances.

One evening when he had taken Mildred Norton to dinner after her afternoon of typing for him, he phoned to ask, "If we pick you up about quarter of eight could you go to see Maurice Chevalier with us? I've always liked that old boy. I understand when he gives readings he has been including some of my poems." I accepted with alacrity. It wasn't at all unusual for Carl to be invited to Maurice Chevalier's or any other celebrity's home. I dressed in my best and put on my favorite jade. The joke was on me! He and Mildred Norton took me to Gigi, a filming of Colette's short story, in which Chevalier isn't even a main character! We went to see Chevalier all right, but Chevalier didn't know it!

Sunday noon, the day before Carl left, he was at breakfast when we heard a guitar and singing in the front room. Alice had asked Bill Clauson over with his guitar. He and Carl had not met since that time long ago when Carl had been so taken with Bill's folksinging at a party here. Carl had been so expressive of his enthusiasm about the boy's gift that Bill had told us more than once that it gave him his first boost up the ladder.

Carl had not liked some of Bill's recordings that had been sent him. He was acting as though he felt he had been rash in his endorsement. I felt a coolness in the air when they met over Carl's breakfast. By the third song Bill sang, however, Carl was again completely won over. Bill was really wonderful. He was thrilled, too, to be getting Sandburg's approval of his work.

Bill arrived at twelve. It was seven-thirty that evening before their session broke up. Alice and I had concocted a dinner while Bill sent for a professional photographer to take pictures of the two guitarists. At one point Carl had laughed, "No one like myself ever got so far as a guitarist on so little! Segovia once said to me, 'Why, man, you've got only two chords!' The next time I met Segovia I held up three fingers and said, 'Now I've got three!'"

It was Sandburg's advice that Bill sometime study with Segovia, that he sometime make a solo instrument of his guitar. "There comes a time in life when a singer no longer sings. Then you would have your instrument with which you have already gone so far. People seem to think it remarkable that at eighty-one my voice comes out true when I occasionally sing a folk song on my program. But I sing soft, I sing low. I sing only once. I wouldn't dare let my voice out as you do."

The day before, Carl had asked me to drive him to Jake Zeitlin's bookstore. Carl wanted a long talk with him. But it was a Saturday afternoon. Jake was intermittently busy. There was no real visit with him this time. On the way home I told Carl that the cooks--Alice and I--not being on the premises to prepare a home-cooked meal, wanted to take him to a quiet little French restaurant that served excellent food.

"Why not my discovery up on Wilshire where you select your food, cafeteria-style? I'd like to take you there."

"If it's to Manning's you insist on going, so be it," I said, "but the dinner's on you then, my man!"

Manning's it was. While we sat in the favored balcony eating I saw friends of mine at a table we had to pass as we left. I explained this to Carl and added, "I would never be forgiven if we walked by their table without my introducing you. Do you mind?" He said some gracious thing in answer and we got up to leave.

The people at the adjoining table had been aware of him. At my speaking his name the woman leaped to her feet and came toward our group, hands outstretched. "This is Mr. Sandburg, isn't it? I felt certain that it was." The others at her table followed. In a moment there were twenty or more people who had been watching our table who were around him, asking for autographs. It was some time before we could extricate ourselves. I could see that he had his reasons for not wanting to eat in restaurants.

That evening, seated comfortably in a big armchair, Carl demanded to have a look at the manuscript of my forthcoming book, <u>Chinese Snuff Bottles; The Adventures and Studies of a Collector.</u> The book had been accepted by Charles E. Tuttle Co., but there were to be a final typing and minor corrections.

After a few minutes of reading Carl looked over his glasses and said with a smile, "Would you think me a fiend if I wanted to put my pencil marks through some of your phrases and interpolate a word here and there!"

"Go to it! Mark it up! It has all got to be typed again." Carl must have spent two hours over those first two chapters, which were all I gave him. It was mostly the beginning over which he worked, the latter part he said he did not want to touch. Any writer, certainly any unknown writer like myself, would rate high such a service. I have carefully put away those pages and their annotations, the penciled corrections and the crossings out. A few I could not use. They sounded so completely Carl, not me.

The goodbyes next morning were as casual as if he were just going to San Francisco. Perhaps we were both remembering that it takes only four and a half hours now to cross the continent.

Los Angeles and Flat Rock seemed all the more like commuting distance when I returned from San Francisco a few weeks later and learned that Carl had returned from the East. Mildred Norton had met him at the airport and he had called my house. He got my sister Alice on the phone. He had further work to do with Norman Corwin, he said, but Mrs. Corwin had a sick child and could not take him into their house this time. Could he stay with us? Alice had to explain that I was out of town and she would not know where to put him. If I had been home I would have said, "Come on over." I could always find a place for Carl in my house. Unaware of Carl's antipathy to a hotel, Alice had no realization of the problem Mildred would have on her hands. Mildred was no longer a newspaper woman. She had married some years before. She told me later that she had no proper accommodations for Carl in her small house. Nevertheless, not knowing what else to do with a man who wouldn't go to a hotel, she did take him home. This I learned when I talked with her later. But his stay this time was brief. He had left town before my return from San Francisco.

Chapter XXII

March 16, 1959

Dear Carl,--
Our L.A. papers say you are laid up with fatigue
for two weeks. Maybe you'll have time to read
your mail--one page only, as you taught me. I
seldom slip on that.
I told you I was a sort of clipping bureau. Everyone sends me any item about you. I loved this!
"A Message for Muggsy." Somehow it seems even
finer away from context; very beautiful. Please
return it, however. I want it for my quote book.
Did you try Paula out on "The two letters"? I
had a feeling you wanted them for her.
Get well quickly. You have a devoted nurse, I
know. I'm not worrying about you. You are strong
as an oak tree still.

Yours,
Lilla

The return envelope is because you're supposed
to be in bed.

"A Message for Muggsy" was a tribute to Carl in the
well-known newspaper column "Jim Bishop: Reporter." It
seemed like marvelous praise to me. Carl did not fail me
on my request that he return it. It came back promptly with
a memorandum to the effect that the excerpt that Jim Bishop
quoted was the only part of the six volumes to appear in
italics.

The clipping began:

187

This is for Muggsy Anderson, 13. He wants to know, in my opinion, what is the most beautiful writing ever to pass under my eyes. The answer is the start of Chapter 72 of Carl Sandburg's The War Years. It concerns itself with Good Friday, the day on which President Abraham Lincoln was assassinated." Jim Bishop then quotes the first ten paragraphs of the chapter, and concludes his column, as follows: "I would stand by this, Muggsy, as the best. It is a small remnant of a great tapestry of poetry, a thing I have read many times over the years, always fondling it carefully with my eyes, then folding it back into the book and wishing I could write like that. I can't, Muggsy, so I do the next best thing: read it.

In June I wrote to Carl about the initial reaction to his having sent Frances and Norman a copy of Always the Young Strangers:

Dear Carl, --
In yesterday's mail came a letter from Frances. I enclose what she says on receiving your book. She may not be as expressive to you when she writes. In the letter from which I cut off this bit she tells of Norman's having received a request from a publication in Bombay, India, for an article on which he is currently busy. Wouldn't it be something if on account of his math articles he were sometime to receive an offer from the institution from which he was kicked out!
Our best to you, and hope you have entirely recovered from your Hollywood fatigue.

Yours,
Lilla

Thanks for doing that for the kids!

This was the portion of Frances's letter to me that I sent on to Carl:

Just this minute received in the mail a copy of Sandburg's latest book, Always the Young Strangers, which he autographed thusly:

FRANCES PERRY

188

For you and your Norman--
With love and blessings

Carl Sandburg

Am I ever thrilled! In fact, I am completely
bowled over, to say the least. Will get a note off
to him right away. We were tremendously pleased
just to get the book, and then when we found the
extra personal touch--it is just too much.

Well, I hope that you will write real soon and
let us know your plans for visiting us.

Much love,
F & N

I wondered if Norman would acknowledge Carl's gift,
too. It seemed as unlikely as Carl's doing so himself, under
similar circumstances, but I thought Carl would understand.
To my surprise, early in July I received an undated, penciled note from Carl:

Dear Lilla:
This was very pleasing to me. Let me have it
back sometime.

Yrs.
Carl

Attached was an almost undecipherable typewritten letter that Norman had written to Carl.

Saturday morning
Perry Cat Farm
130 Cedar Crest Dr.
Auburn, Alabama

Dear Carl:
This is Norman. I completed the biography of
your first 20 years a few days ago, and felt strongly moved to write and tell you how much I enjoyed
it. Like many intentions these days the urge to
write got lost in the shuffle of "busy work," grading
papers, planning lectures etc. and was recalled only
by the sight of your pleasing skit with Gene Kelly
on TV last night.

I have always been fascinated by biography and

189

thought this bit from a Russian writer might charm you by its strangeness.

"As I look back on my early childhood I recall mainly the undifferentiated gray of long sweeps of sensation, interrupted only occasionally by sudden white flashes of perception on which Memory began to attain a slippery foothold."

Your biography echoes all biography. I too was born of love, passion and generation, and asked the question: WHY? I imagine that nearly every family history has somewhere in its annals a Sleeping Mortgage. The Perry family certainly did. I never "sailed on an Illinois prairie," but I have crossed vacant lots in Los Angeles where there grew acres of green grass 3 or 4 feet high. When I was ten years old I thought it was so beautiful there in the bright sunshine that I wanted to cry. At grammar school there was a cute little dark-haired girl with a wide strip of white gray down the middle of it. I was never able to put my feeling toward her into words, but agree with you now "that she was like a flower for which there is no name." There is honest feeling in your memory of Emil who "got tangles in your heart" and honest lack of feeling for Freddie, who did not.

I began reading "the Young Strangers" with a scientific and detached viewpoint. I thought to myself, what are the circumstances which molded this eminent man, whose philosophy of life is so much more optimistic than mine. But as I read I got involved and now I do not know why the same circumstances "make Mary a saint and Martha a sinner."

You spoke of suicide and the bitter and lonely hours so I know that you know the reasons for pessimism and have outgrown them. Yet for me the reasons keep coming back. I began reading a story in the New Yorker last night about a man who visited the Greek island of Salamis, where the inhabitants are abusive to helpless animals, and more abusive to anyone who is kind to them. The story made me feel so bad I had to quit reading and go to higher mathematics for solace. This morning the story resonated in my mind, and I began to be sure that "people are no damn good" and that nothing is worth the inconvenience of effort.

Finally, I had a second cup of coffee and listened

190

to one of my Beethoven symphonies. Now I am
convinced, at least temporarily, that the effort to
be creative is worth while, and returned to my latest background reading for possible research, the
study of mathematical economics.
Well, this letter has been much longer and more
rambling than I thought it would be when I started,
so I will close now. The best of everything to you
and your family and the goats, from me and my
family and the cats.

As ever,
Norman

P.S. This typewriter is abominable and my typing almost as bad, but I think you will be able to
read it.

I was pleased in more ways than one to see Norman's
fine letter, and to know how pleased Carl had been to receive
it. I wrote Carl the following on July 10:

Dear Carl, --
So glad to get your brief note and the enclosure.
Would anyone but Norman have the nerve to send
such an almost indecipherable letter to "the eminent
man. " It shows me that Norman has not changed
much. I haven't had much chance to know as the
letter to you is the second time only that I have
seen his writing since he went down to Alabama five
or six years ago. That occasion was when, instead
of sending him the usual birthday check (from which
I never hear) I scooped up a whole bunch of the
"quotations" I have gathered over long years and
with which you have often been inflicted, thrust
them into an envelope and sent them to him, nothing else. To those I got a long reply, quite Nor-
manese. I, too, have kept that one letter. So if
your word, "return sometime" means there is any
chance that you will want to read this letter over
again, it would be such a painful process that I have
taken the trouble to type it out for you, changing
nothing. The trouble is not with the ribbon of his
typewriter as you might suppose, but Frances told
me, when I jokingly offered to send her a new ribbon, that it isn't that simple, the whole typewriter
is on the blink. She has now resorted to longhand.

191

Are they that poor that they can't get a new typewriter! Gosh!
    All for this time. End of page. You've taught
me letters shouldn't be longer, you know.

Affectionately,
Lilla

    Carl replied thanking me for the return of Norman's
letter and characterizing Norman as a blue-colored cube, with
golden doors, opening and shutting. He felt that I could be
happy and grateful that I had brought him into a turbulent,
ever varied world. He closed by asking me for copies of the
quotations I had sent to Norman.

    The original note, in longhand, I thought Norman
should have and I sent it on to him. It will probably be the
only time in his life that he will have a poem written about
him by a great poet. I sent a copy of it also to Norman's
mother-in-law, Mildred Edgar. Frances and Norman lived
with her, in her house, for almost five years after they were
first married. That he survived such a test and she continued to be so fond of him speaks well of him and of her. She
answered as follows, on October 17, 1959:

    Dear Lilla, --
    So glad you thought to send me Carl Sandburg's
    little poem about Norman. When next I visit them
    it may be stored away in a safety deposit box and
    I might not see it. I am not sure that I get the
    full meaning--the symbols are so unusual. The
    cube probably refers to Norman's being a geomet-
    rician and to his attempts not always successful--
    at being mathematically impersonal. One of the
    "little gold doors" would be his willingness to sit
    up all night helping some poor student with a dead-
    line to make the next day. Another would be the
    casual taking-over of the classes of any other
    teacher who wants to stay out with a toothache or
    a cold although he himself never absents himself
    from classes no matter how he feels. But of
    course the "gold door" I like best is his sympathy
    for animals. He isn't afraid of being sentimental
    in that direction.
    I was in Auburn when Norman received that in-
    teresting batch of quotations. He let me read them,
    and went over them again and again, picking out the

192

ones he liked best.   I know they pleased him more
than a check.
    I did enjoy your letter.   Please do it again.

Love,
Mildred

  Among the quantities of Carl's letters that I saved
throughout the years I came across this carbon of one of my
own that was written on the same date as Mildred's letter to
me.   Carl's continued interest in Norman had led me to write
it.

  Dear Carl, --
  Found your welcome note here on my return
from a flight to Chicago to attend the auction of a
famous Chinese snuff bottle collection.   Fun?   I
should say so!   One of my friends says I am adventure prone and I believe it's true.   But I would
need to have you at your most leisurely moment--
opposite me at a breakfast table--to dare spread
out these latest ones before you.
  Love your little poem on Norman!   If I don't
know exactly what it means, it, at least, suggests
unlimited meanings, and that makes it a poem,
doesn't it?   Norman and Frances were out here this
summer for a week.   They always give us a hilarious time.   Someone asked them how they had met,
a question I had never thought of.   Frances told
the story and I thought you would like it.   Regularly
Norman played doubles while in college on the University of Southern California tennis courts.   Frances used to play with a girl pal on the next court.
As she told it, "I kept noticing that tall, tawney-
haired man and I thought he looked 'interesting.'
He always had a pile of books to which he would
beat a retreat on a bench whenever he had to wait
for his companions.   I used to wonder what they
were that absorbed him so much.   One day the four
of them were standing near the two of us and Norman got off some wild shaggy-dog remark that
doubled me up with laughter, but the faces of his
companions remained blank.   They hadn't understood
him a bit and he shot an unforgettable look of grat-
itude over his shoulder at me.   After that he always 'noticed' me and in gaps in the game would
come over and talk.   One day I said to him,

'Mother and I live over here just across the way, don't you want to come over and have a cup of coffee with us?'"

"That began it," put in Norman. "After that I was like a stray cat they had taken in. I was there morning, noon and night. Frances couldn't stand my late hours and often times she would go off to bed and her mother and I would sit and talk till one or two in the morning." He had found people who could speak his own language. At home he was not finding anyone who did at this time, I remember. He would hardly sit down to a meal with us, preferring to raid the refrigerator for his nourishment. (All to my exasperation I've no doubt.)

"And," continued Frances, "while the devoted swains of other girls would occasionally bring them candy, flowers, or at least invite them to a concert or a movie, Norman never did any of these things. He just came and talked and talked! Once I remember he appeared with a paidup semester of modern poetry which he announced I was to attend with him. I did. We did. And poetry and the discussion of it became the subject of our late hours. Mother had to work hard to keep up with us."

They have told me that their drives around the country sometimes take them near Flat Rock, but they have never been able to get up the nerve to look in upon you.

Affectionately,
Lilla

Quotations? Yes, you shall have them as soon as I can get to them.

Chapter XXIII

It was March 1, 1960. For days now I had been realizing that Carl must again be in town. Phone calls and
mail kept coming for him, and the papers had continuous
publicity about the opening of his show, the one he had made
with Norman Corwin, The World of Carl Sandburg. It had
already toured much of the country to great acclaim. At the
opening in Los Angeles Sandburg himself was to appear.

When he phoned me finally I was not at all surprised
to learn that he had been at Mildred's again. It came out
that he had been there since the previous Wednesday, almost
a week. He called to ask me to be his guest at the opening
of The World of Carl Sandburg that night and to attend with
him the party to be given for him after the show. For time
and place of meeting he turned me over to Mildred.

"The party Mr. Sandburg is asking you to," she said,
"is to be one of those huge Hollywood affairs that my husband
and I would like to skip. Since you will be coming in your
own car could we turn Carl over to you after the show?"

"Why, of course," was my answer. "But instead of
driving Carl way out to Inglewood to your house at that late
hour and having the long drive back alone, wouldn't it be better," I asked, "if I brought Carl home with me?" She seemed
to think so, and thus it was arranged.

There was little to do to get ready for him. I had
learned that two days following the opening he was to take a
plane home. Convenience had thrown him my way for the
last two days of his visit.

I sat at the phone after the call--thinking. Never

195

again would this house be "his home in Los Angeles," as he had so often called it. I had lost him to Youth and Beauty. Mildred was a lovely woman in her early thirties, and he had always liked her. I think as I sat there at the phone table there was a smile on my face--a sad little smile, perhaps, but not too sad. "Conrad in Search of His Youth," I thought. Having once been admitted--no matter how hesitantly into her household--how natural that he should have called her up from the airport on his arrival rather than me. She represented all that within himself he knew to be slipping away, that at eighty-two a man still wants to hang onto--youth, vivacity, energy. What, in comparison, did I, a contemporary, have to offer, with disabilities, no matter how carefully concealed, reminding him of his own. No, I wasn't hurt, just saddened a little.

I turned away from the phone with just a little feeling of relief that I had not had the stimulation of him since last Wednesday, and was not having to pay for it with the complete mental and physical exhaustion in which his last visits had left me. This was the core of my sadness--too sharp a realization, brought out by my feeling of relief, of what old age does to one.

Surely I might once have been hurt. When I, too, had had youth and vivacity, I had had the strength to glory in those mentally exhilarating visits. Would I have relinquished them with the ease of today? I was sure I would not. But old age has its perquisites. The leaf that is soon to fall has its period of loosening from the stem. Nature is kind, in that there comes a time when there are many things about which we cease to care any more. As Carl himself once put it, we "keep away from the little deaths."

When I met Mildred and her husband at the Plaza Hotel that evening Carl had not arrived. He had had a television engagement that day. We sat in the lobby and waited. Mildred was especially lovely in a white evening dress and furs. Carl had two programs for the next day, I learned, and had forgotten to bring in material he was to use for them. That meant he would have to return home with Mildred and her husband. Coming home with me was out.

The big party, however, had been given up. There was to be just a small supper party after the show, just twelve of us. In this we were all going to join.

When Carl arrived I was amused at Mildred. She at

196

once straightened his tie, and practically retied it. She brushed his collar with her hand and asked if he had changed to the clean shirt she had put in his briefcase. Her husband's laughter sufficiently described to me the scene at home when she had tried to cut his hair. "As much as he would let her," he laughed. All these little gestures would have been impossible to me, but I could see how much he must have enjoyed them. There was nothing but a devoted father-daughter relationship between them. This I knew, but it was nothing with which I could compete.

As at every other "first night" in Hollywood there were throngs of people on either side of the theater entrance. When Carl, with his well-known face and thatch of white hair appeared, the crowds burst into applause. Our journey to our seats in the second row was one continuous ovation. My seat was next to his on the aisle.

The World of Carl Sandburg began: a performance consisting of three people reading excerpts from his many books. Bette Davis, Gary Merrill, and a folksinger-guitarist, Clark Allen, carried the show. At first Bette Davis was a disappointment. I had never realized that her voice was of the lightest timbre. How, without resonance, could she possibly express the depths of some of Carl's thought? But I got used to her voice as the show went on. She was the one who carried the humor in it. There was so much that drew laughter that I whispered to Carl, "Perhaps, after all, you will go down to posterity as a humorist!" She gave the poem that ends with the lines I quoted earlier, not "to die the little deaths," and the audience roared with laughter at the way she did it. Carl whispered to me, "There is more than humor in that."

The whole program was well conceived and carried out. There was an enthusiastic audience and the papers later carried rave reviews. At the intermission a line of movie folk came down the aisle to speak to Carl, some to get books autographed. Groucho Marx, Edward G. Robinson, and Kirk Douglas were among the long-famous actors whom Carl knew, but when the new and younger faces appeared Carl could not remember their names.

At the end Carl himself was brought onto the stage. Bette Davis led him to the throne seat that had been placed back of the performers, a sort of symbol, with his guitar upon it, and a pile of books on the dais on which it stood.

Once Carl would have violently objected to this throne symbol, but by then he took such things in his stride. The
standing ovation given him by the audience when he rose from
his throne to speak is something to which he had long been
accustomed, I was sure.

The reception behind the stage afterward seemed un-
ending. The house lights finally began to blink to put us out.
Bette Davis was a surprise. I had expected her to look young
in her beautiful costuming on the stage, but even within a few
feet of her she did not look more than thirty. She must have
been fifty-five. How do they do it?

When we gathered later for our supper at a restaurant
near by, there were just twelve of us, the official family of
the production and Carl's friends. The supper was only mild-
ly interesting. Too many talked at once. There was no
general conversation; no one person held the floor. Talk was
mainly about the show's astonishing reception in fifty-eight
cities up to that time. It had been given to packed houses
everywhere. Financially and in every way it was considered
a success.

When we left we had to transfer some books from my
car for Carl to autograph before he left town. This took so
much of our attention that we failed to say goodbye. Books
had been arriving all the week from people who assumed that
my house was his stopping place.

In the morning just a little before Mildred drove him
to his plane I thought it gracious to call up, I bade him goodbye, and thanked him for the evening he had given me. It
might have been an assurance that there was no hurt here.

Chapter XXIV

On July 10, 1960 the Los Angeles Times ran a headline, "Sandburg to Write Christ Film Story."

John Scott, of the Times's staff, wrote the article.
He had gone down to Flat Rock, North Carolina, to interview
Sandburg about it.

> The tall, lean, 82 year-old man with craggy fea-
> tures and white-thatched head sat quietly on the
> front porch of his rambling mountain home in West-
> ern North Carolina. He was flanked by his wife,
> daughter, and the noted film-maker, George Stevens.
> It was an historical occasion for all.
> Carl Sandburg, two-time Pulitzer prize winner,
> Lincoln biographer, and internationally famed poet,
> had decided to take his first plunge into motion pic-
> ture activity with producer-director, George Stevens,
> of 20th Century Fox, as collaborator on writing the
> production of Fulton Oursler's "The Greatest Story
> Ever Told"--the life of Jesus Christ. The film
> will cost 15 million.
> "I'm taking a high dive that I've never taken be-
> fore. I'm gonna write directly for movies," Sand-
> burg said.
> Stevens, sitting on one side to give Sandburg the
> full spotlight, spoke up in a quiet voice, "Ever since
> I started plotting 'The Greatest Story Ever Told' as
> a film I've had Carl Sandburg in mind as a collab-
> orator. I've made several secret trips down here
> to Flat Rock to exchange ideas with Carl. Today
> we made a deal--no contract, a handshake is
> enough--and I have this great man of letters to

199

share the burden of presenting the life of Christ in a motion picture. "

"Do you consider yourself a religious man?" I asked Sandburg. His shaggy eyebrows went up as he turned, looked at me steadily, then said, "Do you have a definition for a religious man?" While waiting for an answer that didn't come he turned to look at his beloved Big Smoky Mountains that rose majestically on the horizon.

On July 18 the Los Angeles newspapers were full of Sandburg's arrival. I had skipped reading the papers that day. I had no awareness that Carl was in town. I had gone to bed early to read, as I often did in those days. At nine o'clock the doorbell rang. My housekeeper Dorothy Petty answered it and presently appeared in my bedroom. "There is someone here who you will want to see," she said smiling.

"Oh no-oo!" I protested.

"Oh yes! It's Mr. Sandburg!"

I was out of bed before she left the room. I got into an all-enveloping housecoat, and without stopping to even run a comb through my hair, I rushed out into the hall. Carl greeted me warmly. Then to my surprise and a little to my consternation (considering my appearance) he turned to the man who was with him. "This is George Stevens, who's got me out here to do some collaborating with him. He picked me up at the airport today and tonight I insisted he bring me over here. Strange, as often as I've written this house number and been in this house, I couldn't give him your address-- yet I directed him straight to this house. "

"Do come and sit down, " I said, leading the way into the living room. "But tell me, Mr. Stevens, how in the world did you come to choose this old agnostic to help you with the life of Christ?"

In his answer he parried my question, "I've been after him for more than two years. "

"On the drive over I've been telling Stevens a lot about you, " Carl went on, "and all my happy connections with this house. It has always been a stimulating place in which to work. Just now, Lilla, on account of the daily conferences to which I'll have to be accessible, they've put me up in a

200

suite in the Bel Aire Hotel. We'll see how it works out.
But I'll be phoning to you. You'll be hearing from me."

Before they left, an hour or more later, Carl asked
me to show Mr. Stevens some of my Japanese netsuke collection. I brought out my best, of course. Mr. Stevens had
apparently never seen any of them before and his interest
seemed genuine. He struck me as a very genuine person in
every way. "We want to come back," Carl said in leaving,
"some day when we have more time. I'd like Stevens to see
some of your other collections."

It was heartwarming that Carl had wanted to come
over to see me on the very first night of his arrival. But
many weeks went by before I heard from him again. The
papers, however, were full of his activities. He was a natural for newspaper stories. They made a lot about his re-
fusal to stay in a $45-a-day suite in which 20th Century-Fox
had put him up. They compromised by setting him up in a
$25-a-day one. There appeared an amusing article, head-
lined, "Carl Sandburg Scores Hit in Funny Iconoclastic Press
Conference." There were articles about his meeting the
movie stars. There were constant appearances on television.
Regularly I was being called up by my family and my friends,
"Watch television, Channel so and so, your friend, Carl
Sandburg is on." It was evident he was enjoying Hollywood.

In October there came from his publishers a small
book of poems called Wind Song. Then came the October
number of Playboy Magazine with a personal note from the
editor telling me that Mr. Sandburg had requested that he
send it to me and hoping that I would like the way that he had
set up Mr. Sandburg's six poems.

A letter was due Carl for both the book and the magazine and I find among my files a first draft of a letter dated
October 24, 1960.

> Dear Carl, --
> Well, we almost exchanged a book and a maga-
> zine this past month. Only I am not sure that
> Antiques Magazine, in which one chapter of my book
> appeared, ever reached you. And my book, I hear,
> is delayed until December.
> Along came Wind Song from your publishers,
> however. I enjoyed the new poems and the knowl-
> edge that you are still going strong. Thanks for

201

keeping me up on Sandburgiana. I have all except
In Reckless Ecstasy you know.

Playboy Magazine also arrived. I have read the
six poems a number of times. You might have had
them published in any magazine in the world. Playboy was hardly the right setting for them. Considering the one theme throughout the whole magazine
in stories and in pictures you were hardly in key,
were you? Though the editor did try to tie you in,
of course. Note the illustration he gives with "If
You Hate a Man, " a sort of prehistoric creature
struggling through cobwebs with his penis dangling.
Look at your Playboy Magazine and study that work
of art. I'll bet you didn't. Honestly, Carl, you
who can always choose your own spot didn't belong
in Playboy.

The reports of The World of Carl Sandburg in
New York City have been glowing. You went back
for the opening, I believe, and I have been wondering if you have returned to Hollywood. Call me up
sometime. I miss you.

Lilla

P.S. Are they keeping you busy over there in
Hollywood? Some day when you see a free stretch
ahead give me a ring and I would like to see how
you look in your new habitat. According to the
papers you seem to be having fun.

When I meditate on you, Carl, and "The Greatest
Story Ever Told" I recall what Pascal once said,
"One who takes holy water and makes the sign of
the cross will not fail in the end to become a be-
liever. " What's it doin' to yer?

The letter in reply was dated November 10, 1960.
Carl reported that he had enjoyed and took some pride in
having a small group of poems published in Playboy. All the
poems had previously been submitted to Ladies Home Journal,
Life, and Saturday Evening Post, and he wasn't interested in
being published in the literary and highbrow magazines, whose
circulation and payments are small. Harper's and Atlantic
might have paid $10 to $50 for each poem, but Playboy paid
$3,600. He felt that he was not alone in his belief that a
number of so-called respectable magazines flaunted nudity and
sex--magazines like Ladies Home Journal and Life. He also
recalled having Ben Hibbs of the Saturday Evening Post turn

down his "If You Hate a Man, Let Him Live" on the grounds
that his readers might not understand it. He referred to the
Pascal quotation and my apparent fear that he might take up
with religion, and hoped that all these matters might be discussed when time allowed in the writing of Ever the Winds
of Chance. He concluded by mentioning Stevens's pleasure
in their visit with me and hoped to see the netsuke again and
talk with me as though we were at an Old Settlers' Picnic.

My next letter, written on December 11, was in a
calmer vein.

> Dear Carl, --
> It was so good to hear your voice a few days
> ago. We had quite a visit. I am wondering if you
> fly back to Flat Rock for Christmas. Caswell picks
> me up Christmas morning and we drive up to Doro-
> thy's in Ventura for the day. It has been the cus-
> tom for a number of years. Cas provides the
> drinks and Dorothy puts on an excellent dinner.
> You would be invited, too, if we all didn't know
> that the competition is far too great!
> Book out in January. Disappointed that I did not
> get it in time for Christmas. One of the chapters
> is coming out in an art magazine, The Apollo, pub-
> lished in London. One came out in Antiques maga-
> zine here and I am surprised you were not sent a
> copy by them. I requested and paid for it with
> others out of the $50 they paid me. They featured
> it on the front cover. Perhaps in your voluminous
> mail you overlooked it as just one of those things.
> I loved the picture of you taken with Golden--that
> affectionate, amused expression. I am so glad you
> have made him executor of your will, I think you
> said. It means that trust funds for the two girls
> are taken care of. Glad, too, that you have seen
> your eighteen year old granddaughter again.
> I have no doubt that you got the Christmas mes-
> sage from Kenneth Dodson, the summary of the
> activities of the year that he sends his friends. In
> it he says, "The work now in progress is Hawaii's
> Wreath of Love, which should be completed by
> spring and in the bookstores next fall." Shades of
> "Hearts and Flowers" and "The Maiden's Prayer,"
> he can't call the book "Wreath of Love."
> But who am I to tell him that? If you have any
> communication with him I hope you will. But unless

I'm mistaken, his publishers probably will. He is such a FINE person, and such a title would kill the book. He was staying with me while he was working with Hollywood and I wrote down his experiences as he told them to me. I'd like to share them with you some day.

All for this time. Don't forget your old pal. Call me again. Or, as I said, I'll drive over at the crook of your little finger.

Affectionately,
Lilla

Another note from me went out on December 26.

Dear Carl, --

Thanks for having the studio alert me about your television appearance at ten o'clock the other night. It was almost like having a visit with you. I would have missed it, for I am usually in bed with a book at nine-thirty these days. I thought it went over exceedingly well. I'll have to find out when I see you what you have done recently to take off ten years.

Tuttle has sent me air-mail a sample copy of my book. Really I am delighted with it even though the delays in its production have been maddening. The color-plates are beautiful, and so true to the original bottles that it is most gratifying. Can hardly wait to show it to you, though this thrill over a first book must make you laugh.

Yours, as always,
Lilla

Chapter XXV

The year 1961 must have been a busy time for Sandburg. He was working on the film. Through the papers I continued to hear of his activities and a number of times watched him on television. It was apparent that he flew back and forth across the country a good deal. After my one bid for an invitation to drive over to his hotel I never mentioned it again. I was deeply curious to know something about his work. Once when some books had arrived here at the house to be autographed he asked me to bring them over. I could gather from the glimpse I had of his large room that there was much activity going on. His desk and tables overflowed as at his home with books, papers, and memoranda. There was a corner where one could see that his secretary, Betty, an old family friend, whose last name I never knew [This was Betty Peterman (Mrs. Michael Gole), who was Sandburg's secretary when he was with the Chicago Daily News.], was kept busy. The place must have begun to look like home to him. There were no orange crates nor apple boxes to extend his library space, but he had purchased some crude unmatching shelving to hold the overflow. I knew he must have given forth his orders that no cleaning woman was to touch that orderly chaos. There was work being done, plenty of it.

One day he called me up to say that at his request a film he had missed was being run off for him in one of the studios.

"Bring anyone you want to. I could have forty guests if I wanted. "

It was too late to get up a party, but I did have some house guests whom I took. Besides my own group there were

only himself and a few people from his studio. The film itself was one that I, too, had missed, Treasure of the Sierra
Madre. It was a strong film, with not a single woman in the
cast. Three adventurers start out in search of the treasure.
It is eventually found, but their murderous greed destroyed
it for all of them.

Carl greeted me with expressive warmth and we talked
briefly at the end of the show. "Mr. Sandburg is evidently
very fond of you," my friends said. "Yes, I think he is,"
I laughed.

He sent tickets to me when he received an honorary
degree at U. C. L. A. He asked me to drive out to the hotel
and go with him and Betty to a Bowl concert. Andre Kostelanetz, an old friend of his, was the conductor that night.
We met for cocktails at the apartment of the Kostelanetz's
in the Beverly Hilton before the program. It was to be a
popular program, and the Bowl was sold out. Our progress
toward the Bowl, Kostelanetz driving, was a bumper-to-bumper
affair. The opening moment of the program arrived, and
we were not there. Kostelanetz leaned out the window and
hailed a policeman directing traffic.

"I'm conductor at this affair at the Bowl tonight. We
are late. Aren't there any side streets through which you
could guide me there?" The policeman assured him there
were not. "Anyway they can't begin until you get there," he
added.

At last we arrived. Our car was seized and spirited
away at the entrance to the stage. Two attendants made an
opening wedge for us through the throng of people to the
Kostelanetz's box. The preliminaries began. The announcer
declared that there was a very distinguished visitor among
the thousands in the Bowl tonight. Would Carl Sandburg
please rise and let the spotlight reveal him for a moment?
We were immediately blinded with light, and Carl, a somewhat surprised Carl, rose and bowed to thunderous applause.

Kostelanetz gave a spirited conducting of a program of
the almost too familiar. At one point Carl leaned toward me
and whispered, "There seems to be almost everything here
except 'Turkey in the Straw.'" I had long realized that Carl,
musically, had been steadily becoming a more sophisticated
person than in the old days. "Come with us next week," he
added as if in apology, "to an all Tschaikowsky program."

After this first evening at the Bowl there was a gathering of many of Kostelanetz's and Carl's friends in the room behind the stage, which perhaps is still dubbed "the green room." There was much gaiety and laughter. I missed most of it in the babble of voices and for the most part sat in a corner with Betty and drew out her interpretations. Once or twice there was silence created around Carl and he got off one of his amusing stories. Carl still held his own in any group.

On the night of the second program there was a supper party afterward at one of the palatial estates in Bel Air. After both these occasions when I picked up my own car at Carl's hotel (Betty had been our chauffeur from there), Carl seemed as unaware as I that at three in the morning I had a long drive before me. I drove alone through dark lanes and untraveled streets before I reached the safety of Sunset Boulevard. I was completely unaware of any possible danger.

On November 21, 1961, the papers announced that in the book department of one of our stores Carl Sandburg and Harry Golden would autograph Golden's recent biography of Carl Sandburg. I had read the book; in fact Carl had seen to it that the publishers had sent me a copy. I had a feeling that a biography, written by a close friend, had best be written after the man was gone. Otherwise, it lost a certain objectivity. I was sure many other biographies of Sandburg would be written.

I had heard nothing from Carl for some time. I decided to surprise him at this autographing session. I found myself in a long line of people streaming toward a table where Sandburg and Golden sat busily autographing the books. After each signing I saw Carl look up from his writing, smile and make some comment. I waved to Betty who was standing on the sidelines with the store manager. She pointed me out to him and they both laughed. What she said (as she told me later) was, "Watch that woman in the blue coat. She is an old and dear friend of Mr. Sandburg's and he isn't expecting her here. There will be some little explosion when she reaches his table!"

The line of autograph seekers inched along and at last I stood at his desk. Carl was speaking to Harry Golden at the moment and didn't look up as I held out my book. When he reached to take it I held onto it firmly and he glanced up. Surprise and laughter! He jumped up from his seat, reached

out both arms and grasped my shoulders.   He shook them a
little as he exclaimed his pleasure at seeing me there.   We
talked only briefly for there was that long waiting line behind
me.

"I'll be seeing you.   Has a big package of books come
to the house for me?"

I assured him the big package of books was standing
in my front hall.   He passed on my book for Mr. Golden to
sign with some comment which I did not hear.   I joined Betty
then on the sideline and we chatted for a while.   She explained about the box of books.   A friend of Carl's and of
the Kennedys had sent on Carl's books to be autographed for
the Kennedy family for Christmas.   They were to be sent to
the White House after inscriptions had been written in each
of them.   Sandburg would be over shortly to inscribe them,
get them repacked, and have them picked up by express.

Carl seems to have been kept busy with work and play
by the studio.   He knew the books had come.   They arrived
the last of November.   There were frantic letters to me from
the sender in New York, a telegram, and finally a phone call.
Had the books been inscribed by Carl and sent on to the Kennedy family?   I phoned Carl just once about the sender's deep
concern.

A few nights before Christmas Carl arrived with a
secretary--not Betty.   This woman unpacked the heavy box
(there must have been twenty books), and Carl went to work
on them.   The person's name to whom each was to go was
on a slip of paper inside each volume, all members of the
Kennedy family.   I sat beside Carl on the davenport as he
wrote.   After each inscription he handed me the book to hold
open for a moment lest it blot.   I thus got my chance to read
the inscriptions.   They were very fine.   Carl would sit for
a few moments in thought before he wrote.   The inscription
for the books which were to go to President Kennedy (they
were the War Years of Lincoln) was given the most thought
and came out like an inspiring prose poem.   These were moments when my admiration for him was deep.   I kept silent
until he was all through.   He complained because there had
been no book for Caroline.   "I wanted there should be a book
here for Caroline."   I remembered Carl's particular fondness
for his children's books.

Somehow he and the secretary got the books out into

the car. He had arranged to have someone pack and send them for him. Then he came back to talk for a while. He told of the many activities which had kept him busy and of his great admiration for George Stevens. He was now within a few hours of taking a plane for home.

"In some way your book on Chinese snuff bottles has gotten away from me, Lilla. I must have loaned it to someone who did not return it. Do you have another available?"

"Remembering the many books of your own which have come my way I can assure you another of mine is available," I laughed.

When I returned with it he asked to once more have a look at my netsuke collection. "Why don't you write a book on these?" he asked. "It strikes me it's a richer field than your Chinese snuff bottles. You might even make it a children's book and make the legends and stories so often shown in the netsuke delightful to them."

It would never have done to have told him that there had been many books written on netsuke. He would have reminded me that there had been hundreds of lives of Lincoln before he wrote his own.

He looked at each beautifully sculptured piece with careful scrutiny. "Haven't you got some a feller could buy?" he asked. "I'd like to get a few and no one seems to know where any can be found."

"I've a few duplicate types put away for a dealer to take. Would you like to see if there are any among them you would like? You were certainly a wood-carver in some previous incarnation," I laughingly reminded him. "These wouldn't haunt you so if you weren't."

He looked the netsuke over and selected two of the very best. The prices for the dealer had been put on each, and he pulled out his checkbook. I wanted much to give them to him. I hesitated--but they were so expensive. I thought of his $3,600 for six poems to Playboy, of his $5,000 for a twenty-minute reading of the Lincoln Preface, of the heavy sums his agent now demanded for his television appearances. As for me, for these coveted things of beauty I drove an old car, I made a good suit do for more than one year, I did without many things to save for them. Nowadays this expen-

209

diture meant little to Carl, yet I took his check reluctantly. I wondered if he was getting them for his daughter, Margaret, who loved them as much as he did. Christmas was only a few days off.

"No, not for Margaret, not just yet anyway. These will join for a while the little carved dog which has sat on my desk at home ever since you gave it to me years ago."

We said goodbye as casually as though we were going to meet again next week.

How well it is the future is hidden from us. I was never to see Carl again.

Chapter XXVI

The year 1962 went by without any communication between us. I learned only through the newspapers of his activities.

A new volume of verse, Honey and Salt, was to come
out on his birthday in January of 1963, but I was receiving
none of the experimental versions of the poems to be published in it, as I had often done in former years. I began
to wonder if he were angry at me. It was years since there
had been such continuous silence.

Two things might have vexed him--my expressed criticism of his selling poems to Playboy; my withheld permission that he have access to my voluminous journal now in the
archives of the New York Public Library. What he wanted
to see, of course, must have been the portions relating to
himself, which he was sure was among them. They would
help later on as his autobiography progressed.

These two possible rifts in our old friendship troubled
me. His new book, Honey and Salt, would soon be out. He
had been so thoughtful in the past to see that my Sandburgiana
was as complete as possible. If I did not get Honey and Salt
I would know there was something wrong. The date of publication came, the weeks went by, and I got no book. I was
certain now that he was angry at me. It was the first time
in almost fifty years that I had failed to get any newly published book of his, even the expensive four volumes of the
Lincoln War Years. Disturbed by this certainty of Carl's
displeasure I wrote Kenneth Dodson.

His answer was sent on March 30, 1963:

Dear Lilla, --

Letha and I think you should know some things
which may at the same time sadden and comfort
you. Yes, we got an inscribed copy of <u>Honey and
Salt</u> but if Paula had not reminded him <u>we are sure
the</u> book would not have come. This only means
that the Carl Sandburg of 1963 is a very much older
man than your friend of years past.

Kenneth Dodson's letter went on to describe Carl and
Paula's visit with them at the time of his program at the
Seattle World's Fair. His condition was such at that time
that Paula--against his will--made the trip with him. Both
Paula and his agent had advised against that appearance, but
Carl had to prove something. He had to assure himself that
he could still do it.

Dodson and Letha and Paula sat in that audience close
to heart failure not knowing what would happen when Sandburg
came out onto the platform. But there was a capacity audience. They rose and greeted him with thunderous applause.
They took him to their hearts as they always have in late
years before he uttered a word. He fell into the old groove.
He got away with that program magnificently. He read his
poems as no one else can read them. He ad libbed between
his readings with nonsense that delighted his hearers. At
the end the Dodsons and Paula had difficulty in extricating
him from the crowds that wanted to meet him, speak to him,
get his autograph.

Back at the Dodsons' home he stayed in bed for twelve
hours. At no time during that visit was he the night owl he
had always been.

No, Lilla [Dodson continued], you and I will never
get letters from Carl again, but be assured he has
no anger against you. Whenever your name came
up he spoke of you with deep affection.

212

Chapter XXVII

It was the morning of July 22, 1967. I had just eaten my breakfast and settled in my armchair to read. Dorothy, my longtime housekeeper, who takes every household burden off my shoulders, came and stood in the doorway. She has been with me through fifteen years of Carl's intermittent visits. I remember his comment about watching with fascination her making of the bed in his room.

"I drop everything to watch her," he said. "Expertness, swiftness, not one waste motion, not a single wrinkle-- a work of art!"

There was something in her face now that made me drop my book in my lap. "I've got bad news for you, Mrs. Perry. Someone you're very fond of is gone. The news has just come over television."

My hands went out as though I could ward off what she would tell me. "I know! I've been expecting it for some time. Carl Sandburg is gone!"

"Yes, Mr. Sandburg is gone."

I felt Dorothy was reluctant to leave me, but she had an appointment she had to keep. She knew I would be alone all day in an empty house. My sister Alice, who was usually here, was not at home.

But I wanted to be alone. Just at the moment I was shocked beyond realizing that Carl was really gone. I needed time and aloneness.

I felt myself reaching out toward Paula. Should I call

213

her? No, after hours by his side--for she would, I knew, have been right there until the end--she may have found sleep. Some one else would be taking her phone calls. If I sent a telegram it would lie piled up with others from all over the country. It might be days before she opened them. What I needed to say stretched beyond a telegram. An airmail letter would reach her soon enough, long before she cared much to think of mail.

July 26th, 1967

Dear Paula, --

I could have written only a brief note last week when I learned that Carl was gone. But I know that in the difficult days ahead you'll be reaching out for things to help and comfort you. From the volume of telegrams and letters that will pour in you will get the warming realization of how much Carl was loved by many, many people. I can't think of a public figure who was more greatly loved. But in regretting his loss I am going to remind you of our talk when the three of us walked through the country lanes near your house when I was leaving at the end of my last visit. Carl was exploding with what he called his joy in living--in just being alive. Do you remember your reply that he should from now on take life easier. "If you never write another book, Carl, you've done enough," you said. He met you on that. "Yes," he answered, "but don't you realize that much of my present joy in living comes from my writing another book, from my still being able to do the work I love?" Paula, dear, Carl wouldn't have wanted to go on indefinitely with that power gone.

More and more during Carl's later visits to me your name would come up in his talk. One day we were out in my car and I was telling about my visit to you at a time when he was away. "I realized then," I said, "how well you've worn with Paula."

"I like that expression--worn well," he said. "I know I have many times been a great trial to Paula, but she has never had reason to be jealous of me. She may have thought sometimes that she had reason to be, but she never has." And I who have known him, seen him, under so many different circumstances over the years, knew that he spoke the truth.

214

He spoke once on his last visit of the disaster
it might have been had he early in life found a well-
paying job. "I might never have been a writer and
I would never have met Paula." He spoke as if he
were regarding each possibility as an equal calam-
ity. I'm sure that he was.

I am telling you things that deep in your heart
you know. Write me, Paula, sometime in the future when you are able. You, better than anyone
else, know how I share your grief at his loss.

Yours, with love,
Lilla

My eyes were misted as I finished the letter, but there
were no tears. Carl's death at eighty-nine was not a tragedy.
Neither will mine be. We had both lived lives that were rich
in fulfillment. It is natural that we should end. It is tragic
when lives end that never have been truly lived, or are cut
down in youth with great work unaccomplished. Many months
before Dorothy had stood in that same doorway and brought
me word of John F. Kennedy's assassination. That was tragedy on all counts. Not so for you or me, Carl.

I remember well the maddened grief into which the
death of anyone I loved threw me in my youth. No one has
ever expressed it for me except Edna St. Vincent Millay in
lines that I cannot now recall, nor even where I could find
them. But oh, that searing, tearing grief of youth. There
is nothing that in later years so lacerates and sears. It is
fortunate that nerves, heart, and flesh have the strength and
the elasticity then to bear it. For grief then is taken on the
raw, uninsulated soul with none of the philosophy of acceptance that develops in our later years against disillusionment,
disaster, and death.

Nature is kind to the old. There is resignation, or
shall I say acceptance, in us that never existed in our youth.
Probably there is truth in Untermeyer's line, "Only the un-
ripened old fear to die" or fail to meet with inner calm the
death of those they love.

As I marveled over these things I walked about my
empty house, so full of memories of Carl. He had told me
once of his little grandchildren, Paula and John, coming into
his rooms and standing at the corner of his desk. He had
dropped his work and told them a story. Then added, "Soon

215

you will both be gone. You will be downstairs in your little beds, but you will be here, too, standing just as you are now at the corner of my desk." We laughed over that story because John had taken little Paula by the arm and said, "Let's go along, Paula. I think Buppong's getting ready to write a poem."

Forget the humor of little John's remark at which we laughed so at the time. For there was truth in what you said to the children, Carl. You are gone, my friend, but you are still here in almost every corner of this old house. In the early days, before cement walks and garages took over, you used often to sit in my garden, a pad of paper across your knees. I see you now as I once did, with pencil idle and eyes looking off beyond the oleander tree and the bougainvilleas of the tea garden to the far horizon, completely withdrawn into a world of your own.

You are there in front of my fireplace, trying out on us a chapter of The War Years, or reading to us some new poem not yet quite whipped into shape. There is a tightening of my throat as I hear again the rich sonorous voice of your prime, singing to us your folk songs.

Most vividly of all I see you lingering over your noontime breakfasts, sharing with me the poignancies, the ironies, and the ever-welcome humor of life. Yes, as long as I live you will be here in all these rooms.

In them, however, I know you as more than a physical presence. I know you as the source of much of my self-confidence, as a bolstering faith when my spirit flagged, a sustaining comrade of difficult as well as joyous days. Memories, wonderful memories!

"Death will break her claws on some I keep."

INDEX

218

66, 75, 79, 87
Metzgar, Judson D., 58-
59, 60, 79, 96-98, 118,
131-132, 137, 146, 147,
154, 157, 158, 159,
169, 175
Metzgar, Mary Alice, 79,
157, 173, 175
Meyer, Agnes, 162, 168
Millay, Edna St. Vincent,
3, 213
Monroe, Harriet, 3, 7,
8-9, 20
Moore, Dorothea, 12, 14,
17, 25, 28, 30, 32,
50, 104
Moore, Ernest Carroll,
Dr., 12, 17, 32
Morley, Christopher, 48
Mother. See: Simmons,
Emma
Music at Midnight (Muriel
Draper), 114

"Nearer than any mother's
heart wishes," 103
Nelson, Gerro, 114-118,
123, 126, 128-129, 130,
131, 138, 162
Netsuke, 52-53, 126, 176,
201, 203, 209
New American Songbag.
See: Carl Sandburg's
New American Songbag
New Years Eve Flood of
1934, 68
New York Herald Tribune,
150
New York Public Library,
63, 113, 140
New York Times, 171
Norton, Mildred, 120,
148-149, 178, 180-181,
182, 184, 186, 195-198
"Nude Descending the
Staircase" (Marcel

Duchamp), 96

Olivier, Tarquin, 71
Orientations of Ho-Hen (T. K.
Hedrick), 30
Oursler, Fulton: The Great-
est Story Ever Told, 199,
202
Out of These Roots (Agnes
Meyer), 162

Parker, C. C., 39-40
Parnes, Erwin, 120, 126,
132, 136, 139
Pascal, Blaise, 202, 203
Pauley, Edwin, 177
The People from Heaven
(John Sanford), 76
The People, Yes, 62
Perry, Beatrice, 10, 11, 15,
18-19, 20, 38, 54, 55,
59, 60, 61, 79, 125, 158,
173
Perry, Caswell, 10, 14, 51,
56, 61, 63, 79, 136, 139,
142, 143, 157, 162, 168,
203
Perry, Dorothy, 10, 11, 14,
33-34, 44, 45, 46, 47,
51, 54, 55, 56, 145, 146,
147, 203
Perry, Everett R., 3, 4-5,
10, 13, 14, 29, 34, 38,
39, 44, 47, 49, 52, 56,
94
Perry, Frances, 163, 164,
182-183, 188-189, 192,
193-194
Perry, Lilla S.: Chinese
Snuff Bottles, 186, 204,
209; Journal, 36-37, 39-
42, 57, 113, 132, 133,
136, 140, 143, 211; "Lost
Music," 115, 128-129,
130, 131

221